CUBA AND VENEZUELA

AN INSIGHT INTO TWO REVOLUTIONS

CUBA AND VENEZUELA

AN INSIGHT INTO TWO REVOLUTIONS

Germán Sánchez

Ocean Press

Melbourne ▪ New York ▪ London

www.oceanbooks.com.au

Cover design ::maybe
www.maybe.com.au

Copyright © 2007 Germán Sánchez Otero
Copyright © 2007 Ocean Press

ISBN 978-1-920888-39-8
Library of Congress Catalog Card Number 2007928204

First Printed 2007
Printed in Colombia

This book is an abridged English translation of the Spanish-language book *Cuba y Venezuela: Reflexiones y debates* (ISBN 978-1-920888-34-3), published by Ocean Sur.

PUBLISHED BY OCEAN PRESS

Australia: GPO Box 3279, Melbourne, Victoria 3001, Australia
                    Fax: (61-3) 9329 5040 Tel: (61-3) 9326 4280
                    E-mail: info@oceanbooks.com.au
USA: PO Box 1186, Old Chelsea Stn., New York,
                    NY 10113-1186, USA
                    Tel / Fax: (1-212) 260 3690

OCEAN PRESS TRADE DISTRIBUTORS

United States and Canada: **Consortium Book Sales and Distribution**
                    Tel: 1-800-283-3572 www.cbsd.com
Australia and New Zealand: **Palgrave Macmillan**
                    E-mail: customer.service@macmillan.com.au
UK and Europe: **Turnaround Publisher Services**
                    E-mail: orders@turnaround-uk.com
Cuba and Latin America: **Ocean Sur**
                    E-mail: info@oceansur.com

www.oceanbooks.com.au
info@oceanbooks.com.au

Contents

*I cannot be indifferent to the destiny of Venezuela
even after my death.*

—Simón Bolívar

*For sweet lips no cup is bitter;
the asp cannot bite a manly chest;
nor can infidel sons deny their birth.
Give me Venezuela that I may serve her:
She has in me a son.*

—Jose Martí

Introduction to the English edition

After Hugo Chávez was reelected in December 2006 with a clear majority, he immediately announced that a "new era" had begun in Venezuela. He declared to a mass rally of supporters outside Miraflores Palace: "Long live the socialist revolution. Destiny has been written."

A year after Ocean Press published the Spanish edition of this book, Cuba and Venezuela are advancing rapidly, in the new era that began in Latin American and the Caribbean with Venezuela's Bolivarian revolution in 1999.

The cooperation and integration agreements between Cuba and Venezuela have brought impressive results: for example, during 2006, 198 joint economic and social projects were undertaken worth more than $800 million, and overall trade reached the record figure of $2,640 million. The support that Cuba provided Venezuela in social programs continued to increase: Cuban doctors carried out over 62 million consultations and more than 200,000 eye operations. Venezuela provided Cuba with 92,000 barrels of oil per day, and started its energy revolution with the support of Cuba, which has brought energy savings through the replacement of 52 million incandescent light globes with energy saving globes, achieved in just 150 days. Furthermore, 16 new agreements were signed covering oil exploration in Cuba and Venezuela, production of nickel and stainless steel, maritime transport, ship repairs, ship purchasing, insurance, construction and management of hotels, joint production of rice, and an underwater fiber optic cable between the two countries.

In 2007, 350 new projects will be carried out worth over $1,500 million.

Cuba's economy grew by 12 percent in 2006, and Venezuela's economy grew by 10 percent. Social indicators and standards of living of both countries improved at a rate that has been achieved by very few other countries in the world.

The strategic alliance between Cuba and Venezuela and the profound friendship between Fidel Castro and Hugo Chávez have strengthened. Due to the singular characteristics of each revolutionary process, they continue to foster solidarity and the productive sharing of experiences.

The socialism of the 21st century developing under the Bolivarian revolution is compatible with the constant renewal of the Cuban revolution, which continues despite the difficulties imposed on the island by the aggression and blockade of the United States of America.

The new horizon that has been opened by Venezuela and Cuba can be seen not only in the great achievements in bilateral relations and in successes within the two countries, but also, significantly, in effects on other countries of the region.

Examples of these are the electoral victories of Evo Morales in Bolivia, Daniel Ortega in Nicaragua and Rafael Correa in Ecuador, as well as the incorporation of Bolivia and Nicaragua into the Bolivarian Alternative for the Americas (ALBA). These events, amongst others, show that something powerful and unprecedented is happening south of the Río Grande, and that neoliberal policies have failed.

Events like these are so clear and promising that today they are extending throughout the region, prompting President George W. Bush's decision to visit several Latin American countries in 2007.

On this trip, President Bush belatedly recognized the problems of poverty and injustice that dominate Latin America, praised Simón Bolívar and outlined ridiculous aid plans for the region, a maneuver that was counterproductive and failed to fool the majority of the people in the countries he visited, who in a loud voice rejected this demagogy.

In contrast, every day there is more visible sympathy from the people of Latin America and the Caribbean towards the Venezuelan and Cuban revolutions, and more respect for ALBA, which is explained in this book.

Germán Sánchez, April 2007

Publishers' note: This book is an abridged English translation of the Spanish-language book *Cuba y Venezuela: Reflexiones y debates* (ISBN 978-1-920888-34-3), published by Ocean Sur.

Prologue

Venezuela is worth the journey to reach her.

—José Martí

I am pleased to offer to readers of the United States and other countries this edition of Ocean Press, made up of a selection of several speeches and writings about Cuba that I presented in different parts of Venezuela.

I arrived in the land of Bolívar on August 5, 1994. At that time I could not imagine that more than 10 years later I would be experiencing the great satisfaction of continuing to represent my country in this blessed land. It is a great honor to be doing this while the Bolivarian government of President Hugo Chávez, since December 1998, has conducted the most original and promising revolutionary and popular process in our America at the beginning of the 21st century.

What is the relevance of this to Cuba?

The attraction that Cuba's achievements generate in Venezuela has meant that we Cubans are often invited to share our experiences and opinions in forums and the mass media.

In a direct and unapologetic way, I try in those meetings to give each person a better understanding of Cuba, to enrich their knowledge and stimulate new ideas for everyone, whether they are curious or indifferent, and whether they support or oppose the Cuban revolution, which, since 1959, has been admired by the vast majority of Venezuelans.

I have taken the same attitude when I have had to respond to various attacks against Cuba, made sometimes with the intention of involving Cuba in the internal politics of Venezuela.

Those defamatory campaigns have influenced a small sector of the Venezuelan population. This became obvious during the coup d'état of April 11, 2002, when a group of people, manipulated by two terrorists supported by the Cuban-American mafia in Miami, attacked and surrounded our embassy. Inside the embassy children, women and men were left without electricity, water and food supplies. The Venezuelan people and the international community unanimously condemned that action. A chronicle of these events is part of this book [see Chapter 5].

Of course, this is not what we want to highlight. The aim of this book is to support Cuba and its deep links with Venezuela, two nations that are walking together and initiating the most authentic and creative process of integration in the history of Latin America, the Bolivarian Alternative for the Americas.

I feel honored to dedicate these pages to the brave people of the liberator Simón Bolívar. I will be very satisfied if this book helps people in other countries understand my country, which is rapidly growing economically, developing social justice and demonstrating even more clearly its vitality during a new era of change.

I hope this book — made possible by the generous support of colleagues from the embassy, David Deutschmann and Javier Salado from Ocean Press, and especially my wife and children — is received by readers as a modest tribute to the great identity of Cuba and Venezuela, sisters of the warm blue waters of the Atlantic; and to all the dreams and the ongoing guidance of our forebears, José Martí and Simón Bolívar, who knew no borders.

Germán Sánchez

1. The Cuban revolution and Venezuela

And Cuba must be free — of Spain
and of the United States.

—José Martí

Whoever says Venezuela
says America, which suffers
the same evils, which feeds
on the same fruits, which is nourished
by the same resolutions.

—José Martí

In the heat of the changes led by President Hugo Chávez, speculation that Venezuela intends to replicate the revolutionary course
Cuba initiated in January 1959 is steadily proliferating. Those who
promote such a distortion are nearly all adversaries of President
Chávez, who have an interest in creating confusion, and who
themselves are distorted by hatred. It is only on rare occasions —
including on the part of the Bolivarian revolution — that logical
and balanced comparisons between the two nations are made.

This has motivated me to put together this analysis of the
Cuban revolution in its initial, decisive years. It is an attempt to
contribute to the memories of older Venezuelan readers and give
younger ones an overview. It is devised for people who would

like to make an unprejudiced historical comparison between our revolution in Cuba and the process of change currently occurring in Venezuela.

Cuba's revolutionary development in the 1960s cannot today be repeated in other countries of the region. This is as much due to the geopolitical circumstances in which the revolution occurred and the heady speed of its transformation, as to the far reach of key measures it adopted in a very short space of time. The Cuban revolution's unique complexion is located in those factors.

However, that does not mean that Cuba's initial decisions, or the revolution's impact on Cuban society, are irrelevant in the case of other Latin American or Caribbean nations. On the contrary, given that it has been the most complete historical rupture to occur in any country in the hemisphere, the Cuban revolution represents a paradigm—a laboratory of indisputable relevance for the peoples of our region.

This comparison has the objective of contributing information and reflection; it in no way seeks to replace anyone's own thinking or their own process of drawing conclusions.

More than 40 years of socialist discourse in our homeland confirms that the option chosen by Cubans was and is still appropriate.

No revolution in the Americas has generated so many crucial changes in such a short period of time. In less than 24 months, from January 1, 1959, to April 16 and April 19, 1961—symbolic dates in the insurrectionary triumph (marking the proclamation of the socialist nature of the revolution and the first military defeat of US imperialism in Latin America)—profound changes took root, initiating a new stage in the history of Cuba and the entire region.

The Cuban revolution was not conducted according to a precise plan, although the majority of its actions were contemplated in the Moncada program of 1953 (*History Will Absolve Me*). Given that the United States began to clash furiously with Cuba from the triumph of the revolution and the instigation of its first measures, nobody could really foresee how the process would develop. Still, the revolutionary leadership and Fidel Castro in particular had a strategy and clear objectives, which facilitated strong, accurate guidance of the Cuban people and the integration of the revolutionary organizations. Even faced with that forceful, complex confrontation, the decisions of the Cubans were not made recklessly. Years later Fidel summed up the effective formula for the triumph of any revolution in three words: people, weapons and unity. In Venezuela, on February 3, 1999, he put it this way: "Revolution is the daughter of culture and ideas."

Fierce struggle against the domination of the island by the United States and its allies contributed to the acceleration of revolutionary actions. From the early days of 1959 the United States attempted to crush the revolutionaries and prevent the development of the process in favor of the people and national sovereignty. During that year it exerted pressure, issued warnings, and began to organize and execute plots against the stability of the country, the economy and even Fidel himself. In 1960 the great power's plan to defeat its neighboring government and to abort the incipient project of the new Cuba was unambiguous.

In March 1960 the CIA sabotaged a French boat, *La Coubre*, in Havana Bay, killing more than 100 people and destroying the Belgian arms in its hold. From 1959 and more frequently in 1960 aircraft took off from the United States—sometimes piloted by US citizens—to attack the sugar industry, destroy sugarcane plantations, wipe out communities, and additionally, to supply weapons, munitions and other provisions to the counterrevolutionaries. In June 1960 the US president suspended Cuba's sugar quota and in early 1961 he broke off diplomatic relations, banned US citizens from traveling to a country now considered an enemy, and initiated an economic blockade. At the same time, the United States demonstrated its military might by conducting military exercises in the island's vicinity involving 40,000 troops and naval ships and submarines equipped with atomic weapons. On April 16, 1961, it bombed Cuban military airports, and on April 17 mercenary forces trained, equipped, financed and directed by the CIA landed at the Bay of Pigs.

The aggression did not impede the revolution's impetus. On the contrary, it facilitated, legitimized and accelerated the transformations. Audacity, tactical imagination, conviction and a growing radicalization were all part of the meteoric process changing Cuba forever.

Two stellar moments in that blow-by-blow confrontation occurred. When, in June 1960, the United States threatened to suspend Cuba's preferential sugar quota, Fidel declared: "They're going to take away the sugar quota pound by pound and we're going to take the sugar mills off them one by one." In November 1960, when the United States announced that Fidel would be confined to the island of Manhattan during his visit to the United Nations, the Cuban government decided to restrict the movements of the US ambassador in Cuba to the Vedado neighborhood in Havana. Che [Guevara] subsequently summarized this policy with the sharp comment: "One can't take anything about imperialism seriously, that's all there is to it!"

The revolution had no alternative: it could either go to the source of the country's ills, or perish. It had to undertake serious social change and achieve national liberation, or the United States would crush it and impose a more ominous and dependent regime than [Batista's in] 1958. Fidel understood the alternatives most clearly, and on March 15, 1960, affirmed at the funeral of the victims of *La Coubre*: "Now freedom means something more altogether: freedom means homeland. Therefore our dilemma is *Patria o muerte* (Homeland or death)." The anger and conviction of that afternoon gave rise to this emblematic slogan. On June 7, 1960, Fidel developed the concept: "For each one of us, the catch-cry is *Patria o muerte*, but for the people, who in the long term will emerge victorious, the catch-cry is *Venceremos* (We will win)."

Faced with the myth of the fatal flaw of the island's geography, and the power and arrogance of its giant enemy, the Cuban people and their leaders were undaunted. On the contrary, the confrontation gave them strength and resolve. When the United States utilized the Organization of American States (OAS) to support the blockade, isolation and aggression against Cuba, our country denounced the governments that allowed themselves to be subjugated in this way. Those countries subsequently had to face rebellion and pressure from their own peoples.

Those 18 months represented an irreversible historical shift that could never be repeated. Taking the initiative time and again, the fighting people let loose their irrepressible energy until victory was consolidated. As the majority of the poor and many from the middle class gradually discovered, this was the only way they could fulfill their dreams, and no obstacle could prevent the ongoing deepening of the process.

Some elements of the transformation included:

In January 1959 the pro-Batista executive of the Central Organization of Cuban Workers (CTC) was dismissed and a new executive selected. In March, the revolutionary government nationalized the Cuban Telephone Company — after lowering call rates — and the metropolitan bus corporation. Housing rents were reduced by 50 percent and the price of medicines by 30 percent. In May the government approved the Agrarian Reform Act, which abolished the large estates in less than 12 months and redistributed the land either among peasants who had worked it without ownership or by converting it into state-run agricultural enterprises, thereby initiating an agrarian revolution. In July the cost of school books was cut by 25 percent and in August electricity rates went down by 30 percent; while October saw the formation of the National Revolutionary Militias — comprised of workers, peasants, students, employees and professionals—who had begun to organize in March.

In early January 1960 the Ministry for the Recovery of Embezzled Goods—founded by the revolution—confiscated the Fosforero Trust and further reduced the price of 122 medicines. In February, the ministry nationalized an oil consortium (RECA) which had two refineries and confiscated properties owned by the infamous José López Villaboy, including the Cuban Aviation Company, the Rancho Boyeros Airport (Havana) and other businesses. The ministry also intervened in 14 sugar mills and in April announced it had recovered more than $400 million for the people. On June 29, in response to the continued economic, subversive and terrorist aggression of the United States, it took over Texaco, and on July 1, Esso and Shell. In August all US companies in the oil, sugar, communications and electricity sectors were nationalized. In September, battalions of militia troops were organized under the direction of the Rebel Army to fight and eradicate armed counterrevolutionary bands in the Escambray mountains of central Cuba. On September 28, speaking before millions of Cubans in Revolution Plaza, Fidel called for the organization of Committees for the Defense of the Revolution (CDRs) in every neighborhood block, so that Cubans could fight their enemies more effectively as an organized people. In October all the domestic and foreign banks and 382 large enterprises including 105 sugar mills, 50 textile factories and eight railroad companies were nationalized. The Urban Reform Act was passed, conceding property rights to all rent-paying tenants, and finally the remaining US companies were nationalized.

Other important events took place throughout 1960, such as the amalgamation of revolutionary women's and youth groups into two parallel organizations: the Federation of Cuban Women (FMC) and the Association of Young Rebels (AJR). Peasants likewise grouped themselves into the National Association of

Small Farmers and the island's intellectuals formed the National Union of Writers and Artists of Cuba (UNEAC). In April 1961 the revolutionary organizations merged into one political body: the Integrated Revolutionary Organizations (ORI).

This is barely a synthesis of the principal actions of the revolution, which fundamentally changed the way of life of the Cuban people.

Many others could be added. For example, journalists and media professionals took control of the media, placing it at the political, cultural, recreational and educational service of the people. Casa de las Américas was founded, as was the Cuban Film Institute (ICAIC), and the National Cultural Council. Within such a dazzling, iconoclastic landscape, these three cultural institutions represented a formidable structure for writers and artists. The first stage of the educational revolution was launched and succeeded in eliminating illiteracy in less than one year—by 1961—and from 1959 onwards thousands of voluntary teachers took the light of knowledge to remote areas of the island. At the same time Cuba's beaches were opened up to everyone, private clubs became recreational centers, and the barracks of Batista's army were transformed into student facilities.

In summary, during that brief period, the neocolonial military state was destroyed and a new popular, democratic and nationalist government was installed. The repressive agencies of the former regime were eliminated and new defense organizations, based on revolutionary vigilance, were established, with the essential involvement of ordinary people.

Amid such colossal change, the period was also characterized by humanism and careful respect for the integrity of human beings. Due process was respected and followed with regard to violations of law by enemies of the people.

The revolutionary courts punished murderers, traitors and other servants of the dictatorship, and confiscated all the assets of officials who worked under it: senators, representatives, mayors, and party and trade union leaders who supported the dictatorship were deprived of their political rights. Democratic rights were granted to all the people and discrimination against women and people of color was criminalized, in effect creating an economic, ethical and political base for undertaking the construction of a new, free and more egalitarian society.

Fidel's confidence in the nation's history and the attributes of his people, and the people's confidence in their leader, were determining factors in completing the transformation. In January 1959, the young *comandante* initiated his pedagogical crusade in relation to the principles that should guide all revolutionaries and patriots:

> Fortunately for Cuba, this time the revolution will really reach its conclusion... No thieves, no traitors, no interventionists; this time it is a revolution! (*January 2, 1959*)

> The people of Cuba know how to defend themselves!
> (*January 9, 1959*)

> We are a small but worthy people! (*January 9, 1959*)

> If they want friendly relations, they should not threaten us!
> (*January 9, 1959*)

> The revolution is not turning tail in the face of attack, it is not weakening in the face of attack, but it is growing!
> (*January 11, 1959*)

> We are a people prepared for every sacrifice! (*February 3, 1959*)

> The government of Cuba does not want to be an enemy of the government of the United States, or an enemy of any government in the world... but we cannot allow politics to be imposed upon us... Historically we have been victims of the powerful

influence of the United States over our country's destiny!
(*February 19, 1959*)

We can only say to the powerful oligarchy: you have done
what could be expected of you, but we will do what can be
expected of us... Your power does not frighten us, but gives us
courage! (*July 6, 1960*)

The courage of the overwhelming majority of Cuban men and
women was decisive in confronting the serious consequences
of challenging US domination, consequences that included the
sacrifice of lives.

Given the underdevelopment to which Cuba had been condemned, if the revolution had failed, we would have suffered
greater human losses and sacrifice. If anyone should be in any
doubt of that, it is worth casting a glance at certain realities.

In 1958, average life expectancy was 61 years and infant
mortality was in excess of 60 per 1,000 live births. For many years
now, our people have had an average life expectancy of over 75
years and an infant mortality rate of less than seven per 1,000 live
births. How many hundreds of thousands of Cuban people —
adults and children — would have died if the 1958 indexes of
health, nutrition and education had evolved with a trend similar
to the Latin American average?

For a number of years Cuba has possessed the highest per
capita ratio of doctors, teachers, and sports and arts instructors
in the world, and from 1962 its health, education and sports
programs have been totally free for the entire population. Illiteracy
disappeared in 1961 and today the average education level is 10th
grade, the highest in the region. Unemployment, which was over
30 percent in 1958, is now at 3 percent. More than 85 percent of
families own their own homes and from 1959 to 1989, close to two
million homes were built, more than were built in the 60 years of

the neocolonial republic. In Cuba there are no children or beggars on the streets, or unprotected elderly or mentally disabled people. Citizens are far safer than in other Latin American countries, with a very low incidence of social violence.

Cuban people have genuine access to culture. No person's talent is frustrated by a lack of material conditions or encouragement. The revolution created and developed a national film industry that enjoys international prestige, and the fields of visual arts, dance, theater and literature have flourished. In 1989, 100 times more books were published than in 1958.

Sports and physical education are widely enjoyed. For its population, Cuba has the highest number of Olympic gold medals in the world: one for every one million inhabitants. Despite the difficulties of the last decade, levels of nutrition are higher than the average in the underdeveloped countries. One out of every ten Latin American scientists is Cuban and the island has a highly developed scientific research industry, which means it can take maximum advantage of its scientific potential. Its developments and discoveries rate far above other Latin American and Caribbean nations and include many cutting-edge developments in biotechnology and genetics.

Further statistics could be mentioned. I only wish to highlight how the Cuban revolution has presented its people with material and spiritual happiness far greater than the sacrifices we have made. Our people are no longer sucked dry by neocolonial capitalism, or manipulated and oppressed by dictatorship — as during the Batista years and the period under the mantle of a corrupt multiparty democracy. We are a genuinely independent nation — a united, organized nation with an advanced political understanding and weapons at our disposal to defend our conquests. Further, in free elections with a secret vote, people elect their state representatives and depose them if they fail to fulfill their role.

In the early years Cubans never expected that their heroic

actions, or the course of the revolution, would receive external help. The premise of the revolution was that it would defend itself with the support of the Cuban people alone. It should be recalled that from 1959, long before the revolution turned toward socialism, the United States attempted to destroy it and restore the country to its former neocolonial status. It adopted that goal before the revolutionary government entered into relations with the Soviet Union. When Cuba gained allies and began to seek solidarity, it was guided by José Martí's principle that "homeland is humanity." Cuba never, however, accepted threats or impositions of any kind and the Missile Crisis of October 1962 proved the ultimate desire of Cubans to be defeated rather than to hand over sovereignty and the right to self-determination.

Decisions were never conditioned by an opportunistic assessment of the correlation of world forces. Far less were they based on the calculation that Soviet power might become the important ally it subsequently proved to be, although it was undoubtedly significant for the economic progress and military consolidation of Cuban socialism. But our revolution did not exist, and far less act, thanks to the support of that power. When the Soviet Union disappeared in 1991, Cuba stayed on its feet. Despite the brutal impact the event had on Cuban people, they continued forward with their ideals, making necessary adjustments, and confirming that socialism in Cuba is irrevocable. More than 40 years of creatively constructing benefits for the great majority have confirmed for Cubans that this social system was the best choice in those early, defining years.

The Cuban revolution always advanced on the basis of the nation's supreme right to be free and independent. The nature of the political and social system was always decided by democratic consensus. The legislation of those early years expressed an overwhelming sovereign force; it was never passed with less than 90 percent of the people's support. The reason: within a very short period of time the revolution gave people the victories they most desired. It did so ensuring people were genuine protagonists in those victories and the direct defenders of them, thus converting themselves into a collective capable of attaining ever more complex goals.

In *History Will Absolve Me*, Fidel explained the plan of the Moncada assailants in 1953, which was made real during 1959–61:

> We weren't going to say to the people, "We're going to give you everything," but rather, "Here you are, now fight with all your strength so that independence and happiness is yours."

Many other events occurred after April 1961 that consolidated the pillars of the socialist transition, or the shift from a failed neocolonial regime to a more just, democratic and autonomous society. The new human collective, aware of its political and moral force, its cohesion, and the fact that it was armed, lost its respect for capitalist private property and its fear of domination. It transformed these into social property and revolutionary power at the service of all the people. During the clamor, this made it possible for the island to stand as a bulwark against US aggression and the US siege, the longest in modern history.

In those years, Che Guevara published an essay titled "Cuba: historical exception or vanguard in the anticolonial struggle?" Today, 40 years after his reflections, it is clear that Cuba is neither an exception nor a temporary hemispheric accident. Cuba's persistent search for new roads after the collapse of the Soviet Union and the Eastern European bloc, its unequivocal demonstration that authentic socialism does exist in José Martí's homeland — in spite of particular mistakes and enormous difficulties — confirms that this historical alternative is a sound and ultimately promising way to overcome underdevelopment and obtain genuine independence.

At the beginning of the 21st century, it is all the more urgent to find a solution to the drama of Latin America, which endures worse conditions now than at the time of the Cuban revolution. Advances in the living standards of a minority are relative and in contrast to greater poverty in virtually the whole region. Neoliberal globalization and US abuses of power progressively restrict space for countries' real independence. Such realities clearly demonstrate the failure of capitalism in our lands. It is not merely coincidence that, as the power of the region's traditional governments has eroded, leaders and political forces with revolutionary positions (Venezuela) or with a greater commitment to their majorities (Argentina, Brazil and Uruguay) have triumphed. Diverse popular struggles necessary to create new societies are growing.

It is the time to formulate and act on genuine alternatives, and in that process, Cuba possesses many experiences — including its mistakes — that are the heritage of all the region's peoples.

Our people have made huge sacrifices — and will continue to do so with honor — for their audacity in being the first truly free nation of the Americas: for daring to demonstrate that education, health, culture, sports, employment, social security, citizenship, leisure time, individual property, dignity and participation in politics and the economy can be won for all. The Cuban example, even amid the blockade, and with its transitory errors and defects yet to be overcome, has tremendous validity in the 21st century. Furthermore, it stands in strong contrast to the desolate panorama facing other countries south of the Río Bravo.

Even as an example and an undoubted success, the Cuban revolution does not aspire to be a model for other countries: its history cannot be repeated. It is not feasible to export or import revolutions as if they were merchandise. With its own ideas and imagination, and indispensable leadership, each national community will create the forms of its own liberation and well-being, and a political system to guarantee the genuine exercise of its rights. The Bolivarian revolution is evidence of this. In Venezuela, while our bitter enemies seek to discredit and isolate the Cuban revolution, accusing it of interventionism and failure, certain "new left" Venezuelans seem to be afraid of defending Cuba as a historical reference point and of examining its experiences without trepidation.

One understanding that Cuba has gained is in its identification with national history. In 1953, the year a new social and national liberation movement was launched on the island, Fidel Castro claimed José Martí as the intellectual author of the assault on the Moncada garrison. The revolutionary forces were victorious in 1959 — their aim was to vindicate the nation's history and attain the ideals of the generations defeated first by Spain and then by the United States. Assigning Martí that authorial role symbolized the founding of a republic "of all and for the good of all." It was only possible to achieve this with the transformations mentioned above and with much effort, intelligence and skill, similar to that possessed by earlier independence fighters. For Cuban revolutionaries, being a student of Martí in 1953, in 1959, or at any time, means realizing Martí's dream of attaining "the second independence" and creating a republic where "the full liberation of the people" is primary.

The objective in 1868 was to achieve independence. In 1895, Martí included independence within a new and greater aspiration, in keeping with his time: preventing US control of the island and blocking US ambitions of continental expansion and domination. The generation of 1959 maintained these commitments, and in tune with *their* times, went further: socialist revolution, the only way to eradicate foreign domination; to realize Martí's project and humanity's most profound ideas and values. It creatively absorbed the ideas of Karl Marx and those who followed after him, and of all those who embody civilization's inescapable heritage. That generation created an authentic, fertile socialism, capable of recognizing its mistakes and overcoming them.

From the 1960s onward, in conjunction with its ironclad economic blockade and many other acts of aggression, the United States waged defamation campaigns against the Cuban revolution, at the same time keeping silent on its achievements, with three evident aims: to isolate and erode support for Cuba in the international arena, to ensure Cuba's example did not extend to neighboring countries, and to create the conditions to defeat the revolution at an opportune moment.

Venezuela soon became an active staging ground for the US propaganda offensive, and since 1959, some Venezuelan governments have acted as US accomplices in strangling Cuba.

When people in the region decided to rebel against their governments and the dominant classes that were preventing them from exercising their democratic rights — by handing over national wealth to foreign capital, sovereignty to the empire to the north, and by steadily generating more inhumane inequality — our revolution held on to Bolívar and Martí's principle of solidarity with their struggles.

With the exception of Mexico, Latin American governments broke off relations with the island in the 1960s and obeyed the US order to expel Cuba from the OAS. Ten years later, when Cuba had gained international prestige and plans to destroy its revolutionary process had failed, various governments decided in common accord with Cuba to renew diplomatic links, and a group of Caribbean nations that had just attained their independence established such links for the first time. The anti-Cuba policy of the United States suffered a heavy setback.

During that period (1972–75) the Venezuelan government of Carlos Andrés Pérez was among the first to normalize relations with our country. A period of mutual respect and progress in commercial, cultural and other fields began between Cuba and Venezuela. Not long afterwards, in 1976, the criminal sabotage of a Cubana passenger plane, and the impunity afforded its authors [by Venezuela], led to the freezing of relations. During his second administration, Carlos Andrés Pérez proposed their reactivation. From that point, in 1989, Cuba-Venezuela relations have continued to develop, despite certain tensions during Rafael Caldera's government (late 1994 to mid-1995), due to a lack of respect for Cuban sovereignty.

It should be clear that lies and infamies against Cuba are nothing new in Venezuela, but also that they do not have their principal origin in this country. From 1959 the slander campaigns in Venezuela echoed campaigns drawn up and orchestrated by successive US administrations and by the powerful US media. Naturally, they also contained their own lies, springing from an interest in creating problems between the two countries and preventing Venezuelans from seeing how Cubans live and think.

After more than 40 years of US influence in Venezuela and other countries, images, opinions and information circulated about our country have almost always tried to demonize Cuban socialism. Cuba is presented as a dictatorship where hunger and poverty are rife, whose economy is in terminal collapse, where there are violations of human rights, a lack of democracy, citizens fleeing en masse, and where violence is utilized against opponents. Some images have come and gone in line with the times: when the Soviet Union existed, Cuba was one of its satellites; in the 1960s Cuba exported revolution; and currently it is charged with supporting terrorism.

Until February 1999 those campaigns found some popular hearings and local targets in Venezuela. There is the example of the de-contextualized "landing of Cuban guerrillas at Machurucuto" in the 1960s; or the targeting of certain Venezuelans in the São Paulo Forum (a forum of more than 60 left-wing political groups), which has been defamed as a "subversive forum" headed by Cuba and the Workers Party of Brazil. Certain media outlets sporadically published "intelligence reports" spinning falsehoods about the Cuban embassy and Cuban officials, accusing them of committing subversive activities—these campaigns also involved naming left-wing Venezuelan political leaders with the aim of intimidating them. Of course, no one assumed responsibility or could prove such infamies and no government refuted them.

The electoral triumph of Hugo Chávez in 1998 and his inauguration in February 1999 provided a new stage for the anti-Cuba campaigns. During the 1998 elections some of Chávez's adversaries decided to portray him as a puppet of Fidel Castro. They supposed this would cost him votes, believing that the Venezuelan people had been deceived over so many years by lies painting Cuba as a kind of hell, and that they would reject any candidate seen to be attempting to create the same situation in Venezuela. They failed to take into account the history and distinct character of relations between the two countries, or the instinct and wisdom of Simón Bolívar's people. Chávez won.

But they didn't learn their lesson. From 1999 onwards Cuba became an obligatory pretext for the hurling of darts at President Chávez. Even politicians who had previously maintained constructive and respectful relations with Cuba were dragged into sordid, crude and ridiculous campaigns to convert our country into a phantom, present in the background of almost all aspects of Venezuelan life and politics.

Once again, their intention was to prove that Cuba was in all senses bankrupt, and to charge President Chávez and Fidel Castro with acting in league to convert Venezuela into "another Cuba."

In no country besides the United States—and particularly Miami—had such a furious, intense and perverse public campaign been unleashed against Cuba, a campaign, moreover, conducted with complete impunity. They claimed the new 1999 constitution was a copy of Cuba's own, but this colossal lie was promptly deflated, aided by an instructive press conference given to the Venezuelan media by our president [Fidel Castro]. Lies proliferated in the run-up to the 2000 elections. One allegation made by [the supposed Cuban agent Juan Álvaro] Rosabal was that he, along with another 1,500 Cubans, had infiltrated Venezuelan military barracks and was training soldiers. Fidel offered $1 million for each Cuban soldier identified. A few days later, Rosabal himself acknowledged that he had lied.

From 1999 and particularly in the 2000 elections, the most common claim against Chávez involved the manipulation of a speech he made in Havana, in which he used the metaphor of a "sea of happiness" to describe the shared aspirations of the region's peoples. Opponents immediately claimed and reiterated — without ever quoting the speech — that Chávez had described Cuba as a "sea of happiness" and accused him of wanting to bring that "infernal sea" to Venezuela [see "Permission to express an opinion on Cuba," in Chapter 3 of this book]. They wished to generate an atmosphere of rejection of Chávez, constantly reiterating the old lines: "Cuba is synonymous with disaster, it is the worst country in the hemisphere, it is a horror."

In 2001, a large part of the opposition and in particular those who supported a coup [against Chávez], raised on a daily basis the Miami-manufactured slogan of "Cubanization," carrying it to xenophobic and paranoid extremes.

The fanatical authors of this campaign mistakenly believed they could fool people by trying to confuse cooperation between the two countries with the alleged "Cubanization" of Venezuela. They were also seeking to boycott the growing solidarity between the two peoples, which has been firmer and more fruitful since October 2000, when the presidents of both countries signed the Integral Cooperation Agreement. Solidarity has risen to great heights with Barrio Adentro, Mission Robinson and other social missions [see Chapter 4]. A new phase in this process was launched in December 2004, with the signing by Fidel and Chávez in Havana of the Bolivarian Alternative for the Americas (ALBA) on the 10th anniversary of Chávez's first visit to Cuba. ALBA is a project for increased Latin American and Caribbean integration, and is the idea of the Venezuelan president.

During these tense years neither Cuba nor Venezuela have slowed their pace toward understanding and mutual aid. President Chávez and the Bolivarian people have not allowed themselves to be terrorized by pressure or the "sea of lies." These excesses have only found their target in fascist or disoriented groups, groups that went to the extreme of besieging the Cuban embassy during the days of the April 2002 coup, and groups that supported the oil strike of December 2002.

We should be grateful to those individuals who attempt in futile to deceive Venezuelans with the myth of "Cubanization." They are contributing to people's greater understanding of the Cuban revolutionary process. Venezuelans have rejected the image of Cuba as a nation disruptive of Venezuela's internal affairs, and are becoming more critical of the posturing of the authors of such slanderous campaigns. The outcome has been that more people are discovering the essential facts. Not only have people been seeking out objective information on Cuba, but they have also had contact with Cuban doctors and nurses, who provide medical attention freely and in a cooperative spirit. They can see for themselves the professionalism and enthusiastic dedication of Cuban sports coaches, teachers and technicians. They are receiving the benefits of vaccines, medicines and hi-tech equipment from the island. Venezuelans have received only affection, admiration, solidarity and support from the Cubans. That will be the case forever, in line with our sacred principle of respect for Venezuela's sovereignty and self-determination.

I asked the owner of an opinion poll company for his view on the "Cubanization" myth. He had this to say: "When we ask people if they want Venezuela to be like Cuba, most say no." Given his unscientific response, I inquired: "If you did a similar survey in Ghana, the Philippines, the United States, Colombia, or Switzerland, would the response vary?" I answered the question myself: "No people with history, identity, and a love of what is theirs—and Venezuela stands out for these—would allow themselves to be negated and transformed into another nation or character. Venezuela could never be Cubanized—such a thing only happens in media campaigns—just as Cuba could never be Venezuelanized."

Venezuela is and always will be Venezuela, to the pride of Venezuelans. Cuba is and always will be Cuba, to the pride and satisfaction of Cubans. The singularity of each country, however, does not prevent us from describing the multiple similarities and relationships between our two communities. It must also be said that the overwhelming majority of Latin Americans are less concerned about "Cubanization" than they are about the subjection of their countries to the United States and to transnational capital.

Our two nations have much in common and their historical links and reciprocal influences are irreversible. Relations between the two countries go beyond present circumstances and interests. History cannot be erased.

Who could erase from our people's memory the fact that Simón Bolívar's first nurse was the Cuban Inés Mancebo López? Can it be forgotten that Bolívar and Antonio José de Sucre wanted to make Cuba independent, and that after the battle of Ayacucho, both planned for this idea and sought international support for the project? Or that the Cuban national education system was conceived and promoted by the Venezuelan Narciso López? Cuban blood flowed in Sucre's veins, from his Cuban grandfather, and the blood of General Antonio Maceo's Cuban mother and Venezuelan father Marcos (who, moreover, died in combat in 1868 fighting for Cuba's freedom) ran and mingled in his veins. It is impossible to erase the signing of Venezuela's act of independence (1811) by Cuban Francisco Javier Yanes, who at the age of 23 died in Venezuela and whose remains were laid to rest in the national mausoleum. It will always be to the pride of our nations that a group of Cubans joined the Venezuelan Liberation Army, took part in the battles of Carabobo and Ayacucho, and that various children of this Bolivarian land fought and died in the struggles for Cuban independence, among them some outstanding officers.

It cannot be forgotten that during the Cuban wars of independence Venezuelan governments and citizens offered support in the form of arms and troops and entire expeditions left for the island from here. Who could underestimate the decisive impact on the genius José Martí's political formation of the six months he spent in Caracas? Or the wide influence he had on an entire Venezuelan generation, who viewed him as a young redeemer of our America and an illustrious poet, who wrote the first modernist text in Venezuela and later pronounced unparalleled words on Simón Bolívar? We cannot forget the fact that the Venezuelan Colonel Carlos Aponte died in Matanzas alongside Antonio Guiteras, the revolutionary Cuban fighter, as they were preparing to travel to Mexico to organize an armed expedition to combat the first Batista dictatorship in 1948. Or the fact that Rómulo Gallegos lived in exile in Havana after his defeat in 1948, or that other anti-dictatorship combatants like the poet Andrés Eloy Blanco, great-grandson of the composer of the Cuban national anthem, also found refuge in Cuba.

Is it possible to overlook the reciprocal links and influences in the culture of the two peoples? From the first Cuban national poet José María Heredia, who lived in Caracas for five years and on leaving the city at the age of 13, wrote an elegy to the city; to Alejo Carpentier, the greatest Cuban novelist of the last century, who wrote many of his rich works in and inspired by this land of grace, as did José Martí, Nicolás Guillén and other Cuban poets, artists, and intellectuals. Rómulo Gallegos wrote his novel *La Brizna de Paja en el Viento* (The Straw in the Wind) in Cuba. There are Andrés Eloy's memorable poems and Cuban articles; there is Miguel Otero Silva, brother of Carpentier and Guillén in everything, who left us his moving poem, "I do not know Cuba," written in Caracas but giving the impression that he had always lived in Cuba, where he had not yet even traveled.

Who can surpass the finest interpretation outside Venezuela of Simón Díaz's song, "Caballo Viejo" (Old Horse), by the Cuban Barbarito Diez? Isn't Oscar de León the most authentic student of Benny Moré outside Cuba? What is the mystery in the fact that Venezuelans still joyfully recall the only baseball game in which they beat Cuba—in 1941? Why is it so common for Cubans and Venezuelans to fall in love and create families? How many Venezuelans travel to the island every week to become *santeros* and accept godparents there? It should be added that Venezuela is one of the Western countries to most appreciate—and dance to—a Cuban *bolero* or *son*. It holds Pablo Milanés, Silvio Rodríguez and the New Song Movement in great admiration. Cuban children begin to learn the history of our America by reading José Martí, who tells them in *La Edad de Oro* (The Golden Age) who Simón Bolívar was and why they should respect him and follow in his footsteps.

So much important history unites the two countries. Just 22 days after the triumph of the Cuban revolution, on January 23, 1959, Fidel Castro traveled to Caracas to thank Venezuelans for the generous solidarity they had demonstrated: "You gave us heart during the struggle with your sympathy and affection. You saw to it that Bolívar came to the Sierra Maestra."

It is clearly not unusual that in present times Venezuela should include Cuba in an energy agreement which benefits all countries in the Caribbean, or that Cuban doctors are working for the health of millions of poor Venezuelans, or that sports teachers from the island are helping to develop a culture of physical education in Venezuela, or that our educational advisors are working on literacy programs and mass training courses, or that Cuban sugar technicians are immersed in advancing that sector.

The Integral Cooperation Agreement between the two nations was an evolution of those relations. Prior to 1999, Venezuela was Cuba's prime trade partner in the region and its principal oil supplier. For Venezuela, the island was an excellent collaborator in the fields of social economy, science and technology. The decision of the two governments in December 2004 to sign a historic agreement initiating bilateral integration (ALBA), with the perspective of transforming the ideas of Bolívar and Martí into reality, represents a new stage in the continental struggle for emancipation, emphasizing the need for unity and a greater compromise on the part of both nations.

Manuel de Quesada, a general in our first war of independence, wrote in Caracas in May 1871: "Here I have discovered for Cuba the sympathy of brothers, the faith of compañeros, and the enthusiasm of those who feel they are living Cuba's glories." He observed: "The people of Venezuela are Cubans for the love they profess for us."

Martí felt the same 10 years later, exclaiming: "Let Venezuela tell me in what way I can serve her; she has in me a son!"

That is what all Cubans feel today. By devoting ourselves to Venezuela and modestly giving that nation as much as we can to alleviate its pain and contribute to its happiness, we are doing no more than reducing to some extent the debt of gratitude we will always have to its people.

Finally, it is important to emphasize the enormous force emanating from the current Bolivarian revolutionary process.

Let us compare what occurred in Cuba from 1959 to 1961 and events in Venezuela from February 2, 1999, to date. The Cuban revolution was initiated by young civilians who assaulted two military garrisons on July 26, 1953, in order to arm the people and defeat a murderous military dictatorship. In Venezuela it was the reverse: a group of young soldiers rebelled on February 26, 1992, and sought to defeat a civil government and a democratically elected regime they believed had gone rotten. The Cuban revolution triumphed on January 1, 1959, the result of a popular war that defeated the armed forces of the dictatorship. In Venezuela, the revolutionary process began on December 6, 1998, with the presidential election of Hugo Chávez at the ballot boxes. The Cuban revolution radically transformed the state and its capitalist system of ownership. In Venezuela changes are advancing without alterations to the system of capitalist ownership or the essence of the liberal political system. A cursory comparison of the constitutions of both countries defeats the media lie regarding Venezuela's "Cubanization."

The grandeur of any historical phenomenon comes from its own profile and ultimately from the connection between its roots and its contemporary actions. The Cuban revolution was able to succeed and consolidate itself on account of its indigenous nature and its creativity. The Bolivarian process is genuine because it is likewise autonomous and creative and is moving forward without hesitation toward its goals of equality, the emancipation of the poor, democracy for all and full self-determination. The two revolutions coincide on one point: neither of them follows a foreign model.

The Bolivarian revolution continues advancing in its own original direction, without shying away from confrontations provoked by the imperialist government in Washington and its regional allies, who are acting together in attempts to prevent the achievements and growing consolidation of the revolutionary process. In February 2004, addressing a huge popular gathering in Caracas, President Chávez defined the anti-imperialist nature of the Bolivarian revolution, and one year later, in February 2005, affirmed that the only alternative to capitalism is socialism, calling on Venezuelan revolutionaries and the rest of the world to create the new socialism of the 21st century.

At this stage, it is not possible to definitively assess a revolution that is so young and forceful. Especially not when its unique leader—forged from Venezuela's wise history and with a lucid vision of his continental and global role—has decided to act on a catch-cry charged with meaning, as much for its author Che Guevara as for his own confrontation with the dominant world system: *"Hasta la victoria siempre!"* ("Ever Onwards to Victory!")

In prioritizing the search for and the implementation of anti-capitalist alternatives, Chávez is adopting a strategy proposed in other countries many years ago. Cuba initiated such a strategy in circumstances that will not repeat themselves. In Chile, the United States and its fascist Chilean accomplices destroyed the experiment led by Salvador Allende in the 1970s. Since then, no other Latin American leader has publicly declared that socialism is the only possible option for replacing capitalism. In that context it is the task of the Bolivarian revolutionaries of Venezuela to visualize and implement the forms of that specific socialism promoted by Chávez, based on the constitution approved by the people in December 1999.

In pursuit of the well-being, independence and sovereignty of their countries and of all of the Americas, the leaders of Venezuela and Cuba are forging ahead to create mutual cooperation and understanding. This is in total accordance with the two nations' history of solidarity and affection, and in spite of pressure to separate the two peoples. In this context, Cuba will become steadily more Venezuelan and Venezuela will have Cuba much closer and more disposed to fulfill Martí's mandate: "Let Venezuela tell us in what way we can serve her."

ALBA, a new model of integration for Latin America, in which economies can advance and complement each other, is appearing in the *barrios* and remote areas of Venezuela, where Cuban doctors are attending to 17 million people and where millions of people previously excluded from education are learning to read and write, or are reaching higher levels of education with the methods and support of Cuba. At the same time, President Chávez has included Cuba in Venezuela's cooperative energy policy for other countries in the region.

ALBA and its implementation accord represent the culmination of the intensive cooperation instigated at the end of 2000 in almost all economic and social sectors. The historic agreement between the two governments launches a new phase in bilateral relations, currently directed toward concrete acts of integration. The two nations are increasing the exchange of goods and services in order to have a direct and tangible impact on economic and social development and the material and spiritual lives of their citizens.

Under the agreement, which is going ahead at full speed, both countries are drawing up strategic plans to guarantee productive complementation; to exchange essential technologies developed by either side; to work with other countries by common consent to eliminate illiteracy; to collaborate on health programs to the benefit of other peoples; to make mutually beneficial investments under the same terms as national agencies and to develop various association models; to open subsidiaries of state-owned banks in both countries; to sign a reciprocal credit agreement; and to develop joint cultural projects.

The agreement takes into account the political, economic, social and legal asymmetries between the two countries, noting that the blockade and aggressions suffered by Cuba give the island much less flexibility in its foreign economic policy. Venezuela belongs to institutions of which Cuba is not a member, and that reality should be respected in applying the principle of reciprocity in trade and finance.

Consequently, Cuba proposed and Venezuela accepted the adoption of various decisions to contribute to rapid bilateral integration:

1. Cuba will immediately eliminate tariff and non-tariff barriers on all imports from Venezuela.

2. All Venezuelan state or joint ventures and private capital investment in Cuba are to be exempt from taxes on profits during the period of the recovery of the investment.

3. Cuba will grant to vessels flying the Venezuelan flag the same treatment given to vessels flying the Cuban flag in all operations in Cuban ports.

4. Cuba grants Venezuelan airlines the same facilities enjoyed by Cuban airlines in regards to passenger transportation, freight to and from Cuba, and airport services and facilities, including for services within Cuban territory.

5. The price of oil exported from Venezuela to Cuba is to be fixed on the basis of international market prices, as stipulated in the current Caracas Agreement in force between the two countries. Bearing in mind the traditionally volatile nature of oil prices, which on occasions has seen the price of Venezuelan oil fall beneath $12 per barrel, Cuba offers Venezuela a guaranteed price of no less than $27 per barrel, always in conformity with the commitments assumed by Venezuela within the Organization of the Petroleum Exporting Countries (OPEC).

6. In relation to investments by Venezuelan state entities in Cuba, Cuba eliminates any restriction on the possibility of these being 100 percent the property of the Venezuelan state investor.

7. Cuba will offer 2,000 scholarships per year to young Venezuelans to engage in advanced studies in any area deemed of interest to Venezuela, including scientific research.

8. The import of Cuban goods and services can be paid for with

Venezuelan goods, in Venezuelan national currency, or in other mutually acceptable currencies.

9. In relation to sporting activities that have become so important for the Bolivarian process in Venezuela, Cuba offers the use of its facilities and anti-doping equipment, under the same conditions that are granted to Cuban athletes.

10. In the education sector, exchange and cooperation is to be extended to all teaching methods, programs and techniques of interest to Venezuela.

11. Cuba places at the disposal of the Bolivarian University the support of more than 15,000 medical professionals participating in Barrio Adentro, to train as many doctors and health specialists, including candidates for science degrees, as Venezuela needs. Our doctors will also support all those students in Mission Sucre who wish to study medicine and graduate as doctors — who could number tens of thousands within 10 years.

12. The primary health services offered by Cuba within Barrio Adentro — to more than 15 million people — will be provided on highly preferential terms to be mutually agreed.

13. Cuba is to facilitate multi-destination tourism packages from Venezuela, without fiscal charges or restrictions of any other type.

In its turn, Venezuela proposed — and Cuba happily accepted — the following actions toward accelerated bilateral integration with the island:

1. The sharing of Venezuela's technology in the energy sector.

2. Venezuela will eliminate tariffs or non-tariff barriers on all Cuban imports to Venezuela.

3. Any Cuban state or joint venture in Venezuela is to be exempt from taxes during the period of recovery of the investment.

4. Venezuela is to offer scholarships to Cuba for studies in the energy sector and any others of interest to Cuba, including in research and science.

5. Venezuela is to provide funding for construction or infrastructure projects in the sectors of energy, electricity, road reconstruction and other roads administration projects, the development of ports, aqueducts, drainage systems and agribusiness, among others.

6. Venezuela is to offer tax incentives for projects of strategic interest to the [Cuban] economy.

7. Venezuela is to grant preferential facilities to vessels and aircraft flying the Cuban flag in Venezuelan territory within the limits of its legislation.

8. Venezuela is to facilitate multi-destination tourism packages from Cuba without fiscal charges or restrictions of any other type.

9. Venezuela is to place its air and maritime transportation infrastructure and equipment at Cuba's service, on preferential terms, in order to support Cuba's economic and social development.

10. Venezuela is to offer facilities to establish joint ventures with Cuban capital to process raw materials.

11. Venezuela is to collaborate with Cuban biodiversity research.

12. Venezuela is to accept Cuban participation in the bilateral consolidation of state-run initiatives and cooperatives.

13. Venezuela is to develop agreements with Cuba in the sphere of telecommunications, including the use of satellites.

What happened after these historic documents were signed?

Immediately, ministerial representatives of both governments — along with hundreds of officials and technicians, under the personal direction of the two presidents — began work, first separately and then in coordination, over four months. They developed a whole range of actions and ideas to transform the proposals of December 14, 2004, into reality.

On April 27–28, 2005, the First Cuba-Venezuela Meeting for the Application of ALBA took place in Havana, with Fidel, Chávez, 17 Venezuelan ministers and their Cuban counterparts.

One event organized by the two governments for the occasion—which became top news—was a large exhibition of Venezuelan goods, bringing to Havana 150 Venezuelan business representatives and cooperative members, many of them exporting for the first time. This was a most original and immediate result of integrating the two economies. Cuba decided to prioritize purchases on the Venezuelan market and immediately directed $200 million to that end, matched by a further $200 million in credits granted to the island by the Bolivarian government. In the framework of the exhibition an agreement was signed in the presence of both presidents, announcing that $412 million had been set aside to begin purchasing from Venezuelan producers, especially in the private sector, and anticipating that within one year that sum would rise to $1 billion with the possibility of directly generating 100,000 jobs in Venezuela.

The most important agreements of the government meeting itself include:

- In 2005, the inauguration in Venezuela of 600 general diagnostic centers (CDIs) and intensive care and emergency services; 600 rehabilitation and physiotherapy rooms; and 35 hi-tech medical centers offering free, professional health services to the entire Venezuelan population. Cuba will acquire the medical equipment and guarantee its functioning, with the support of more than 10,000 professionals.

- To train 40,000 doctors and 5,000 health specialists in Venezuela within Barrio Adentro II. A further 10,000 young Venezuelans are to study medicine in Cuba, living throughout the country in the homes of Cuban families.

- Cuba will continue its contribution to Barrio Adentro I and II, with the participation of more than 30,000 Cuban doctors and other health workers throughout the territory of Venezuela.

- In 2005, 100,000 Venezuelans will undergo surgery in Cuba for various eye disorders. In the second half of 2005, Venezuela and Cuba are to extend Mission Milagro to other Latin American countries, thereby enabling tens of thousands of people with vision problems — but without resources — to receive these benefits.

At the same time, Cuba will maintain its contribution to the other Bolivarian social programs, including Mission Robinson I, through which Venezuela will soon declare itself the second country free of illiteracy in the Americas. In addition, both nations are to work on designing a continental project to eliminate illiteracy in Latin America and the Caribbean.

The presidents of both countries opened an office of the Venezuelan state oil company, PDVSA-Cuba, in Havana, the objective of which is the exploration and exploitation, refining, import, export and marketing of hydrocarbons and their derivatives, as well as their transportation and storage.

A 100 percent Venezuelan-owned branch of the Industrial Bank of Venezuela was opened in Havana, and the imminent opening of a 100 percent Cuban-owned branch of the Foreign Bank of Cuba in Caracas was agreed. Both state institutions will make a sustained contribution to strengthening economic relations and bilateral trade, which is already beginning to materialize.

The third meeting of the administrative commission of the Economic Complementation Agreement took place, which agreed to grant preferential tariffs to 104 new export lines to Cuba and established a time period for progressive tax relief both for these and existing preferentials.

Cuba exempted Venezuelan imports from customs duties. Cuba also exempted taxes on profits for priority enterprises and for those ships flying the Venezuelan flag and involved in the transportation of passengers or cargo to its national territory, as well as exempting the payment of tonnage fees for Venezuelan ships arriving in Cuban ports from other countries.

Both delegations signed on 11 joint enterprise projects and other models of economic cooperation in Cuba and Venezuela, to be formalized in stages. These include: establishing a strategic alliance to develop Venezuelan iron, steel and heavy industry; a joint enterprise to recover and exploit raw materials; a joint enterprise to upgrade the railroad infrastructure of both countries; promoting integration in the area of maritime transportation; a joint enterprise to promote agricultural development; the exploitation of the Matanzas fuel deposit; a strategic alliance to develop nickel and cobalt mining projects; the building and repair of vessels of either state; the manufacture of sports items; a joint enterprise in fuel transportation; and a joint enterprise to construct housing and social projects in Venezuela, Cuba and other countries.

The organization of nine endogenous economic development projects in both countries was also agreed on.

More than 50 agreements, framework contracts and memorandums of intent were signed in relation to air and maritime transportation; the construction and use of a naval repair shipyard and the building of small naval units; plant and animal health; tourism; information technology; transportation; communication; hydraulic resources; the buying and selling of fuel and the storage of crude oil and its derivatives; the restoration of the Cienfuegos refinery by PDVSA (the Venezuelan state oil company) and CUPET (Cuba Petroleum); cooperation in the sphere of the electrical industry and in the energy sector; the convening of the first Latin American and Caribbean Integrated Games to take place in Cuba from June 17–30, 2005; the promotion of ALBA to international agencies by the foreign ministries of both countries; and a cultural cooperation program covering publishing, film and the music industry, plus a study into the further creation of joint enterprise cultural industries.

This strategic plan is a flexible instrument to be expanded and enriched in line with new proposals that meet the objectives of ALBA and its implementation accord.

Faced with these tangible results and the surge of ideas, President Chávez exclaimed: "Never before have we advanced so far in such a short time! A great day for our America has arrived, let us make it possible!"

The spectacular, solid achievements of ALBA in its first examples from Cuba and Venezuela have aroused increasing concern and intrigue from the empire in the North and its powerful servants in the South. That empire has suffered the further defeat of failing to implement the Free Trade Area of the Americas (FTAA) in January 2005, prompting Chávez and Fidel at the Havana meeting to declare — as a statement of fact — its demise.

Thus, in the first years of the 21st century, with their respective examples of solidarity, strength and dignity, Venezuela and Cuba have become the most vigorous force toward the definitive liberation and union of all peoples south of the Río Bravo.

2. Contemporary Cuba

Cuba does not go borrowing
throughout the World: it goes as a sister
and works with the authority of one.
By saving itself, it saves.
Our America will not fail her, because she will not fail America.

—José Martí

Cuba and the crisis of socialism

1994 was a historic year for Cuba: the economic crisis that exploded in 1991 touched bottom and the country made a slight recovery. It is still not the time for a balance sheet and less still for prognostications. The turbulence makes it difficult to see the recent past with clarity, or to fully envisage the future. It is, however, possible to express various certainties.

Why has Cuba been able to resist and survive that tremendous crisis? What point have we now reached? Is it the terminal phase of Cuban socialism, or are we beginning to emerge from the most extreme critical stage?

We are in the midst of the most brutal crisis to have hit the island in the present century. Its impact has been heartrending in terms of the economy and the everyday life of the people. But it has not led to the death of socialism. In spite of the difficulties, the mistakes and the uncertainties in the hearts of the people, they have held firm under the leadership of a consistent political vanguard. United, we undertook various actions that allowed us to negotiate huge obstacles, to preserve the principal achievements of the revolution, and to adapt ourselves to tremendous international changes and begin to put together the jigsaw puzzle of a new stage of national history.

In order to achieve that the Cuban government rooted its credibility in the formidable benefits the revolution has brought to the people over more than 30 years, and in its capacity to confront vicissitudes and failures with serenity and the creative participation of the people.

Socialism brought a new way of life to the Cuban people. A genuinely free and independent people with a dignified and proud identity arose.

Whereas in 1959 the average life expectancy was barely 61 years, by 1989 it was in excess of 74 years. And whereas in 1959, 60 infants per 1,000 live births did not survive, in 1989 only 11 died.

Other spectacular advances have occurred in education, sports and culture, placing Cuba at the level of many of the developed countries. By 1989 more than 85 percent of families owned their own homes, and telephone and electricity charges were among the cheapest in the world; education and health care — of high quality and within the reach of everyone — were free; social security was guaranteed; unemployment was minimal; nutrition levels high; and the people enjoyed sport, recreation and culture at mass levels.

Notable economic advances sustained all those social achievements. For example, while Latin America stagnated in the 1980s (the so-called lost decade), Cuba experienced a 33 percent growth in per capita GDP.

Thus, when the disintegration of the Soviet Union and Eastern Europe occurred, the regime in Cuba was enjoying good health:

the economy was developing satisfactorily (although naturally not without problems and errors) and the quality of life shared by all Cubans was superior to that elsewhere in Latin America.

A factor that allowed Cuba to face the crisis after the collapse of Soviet socialism was that in 1986 the government embarked on a process of "rectifying errors and negative tendencies," in order to divest the Cuban system of errors and deformations originating from the ill-named "real socialism" [of the Soviet Union]. It is a fact that we had copied the Soviets and in doing so we erred. We became aware of that by observing economic inefficiency, the squandering of resources, excessive material incentives that exacerbated individualism, expressions of privilege within the technical classes, ritualism in political undertakings, and partial imitation in the teaching of Marxist theory — among other mistakes. The process of rectifying those errors began in 1986, and functioned as an antidote against the disintegrative components of socialism applied in the Soviet Union and the rest of the Eastern European bloc. There, after several decades of committing arbitrary actions, multiplying deformations and justifying everything in the name of "real socialism," a means of avoiding collapse was sought in perestroika, which provoked a fatal fall into the precipice.

Cuban socialism was not perfect or exempt from deficiencies, but it continued to be essentially healthy and it had the potential to adequately confront and overcome its deviations and errors. Many of these were derived from the incorporation of the models of the European countries into the system of directing the economy, and in some political aspects and the teaching of Marxism during the period 1975–86.

However, in Cuba the errors did not have a strategic reach and were opportunely and publicly criticized by the country's leadership, particularly Fidel. In the face of the mistakes solutions were sought that did not affect national and revolutionary unity, thus elevating morale and popular participation even higher.

Having survived the profound economic crisis, Cuba was able to exhibit tangible successes in all spheres of society. Our people knew that only socialism had been capable of providing them with those monumental changes in their way of life, and that such conquests could be preserved by defending their principles and values and resisting temporary setbacks. Of course, the impact of the disintegration of the Soviet Union and the other socialist countries hit the Cuban economy with the force of a cyclone: apart from tourism and oil production, all sectors contracted with an average decrease of around 34 percent of GDP up to 1993. Imports fell by 79 percent, the fiscal deficit reached 35 percent and the dollar exchange rate on the parallel market rose to 120-plus pesos. Nights without electricity, a brutal collapse in transportation and food consumption, and other vicissitudes of various kinds gravely affected the daily life of all Cuban citizens.

This debacle also provoked questions and political, ideological and historical debates within a large part of the population. In a short space of time (1989–91) Cubans saw the loss of their "strategic allies" and with it the shattering of myths and dogmas such as the "irreversibility of socialism" and the "indestructible friendship of the Soviet Union."

A neighboring "bird of prey," the government of the United States, thought that it would soon be able to devour the corpse of socialism on the island. On noticing that Cuban life was continuing, it lost no time in acting with all the vast potential of an empire that had conquered the world.

In the 1960s—in the wake of the Bay of Pigs and the October Missile Crisis—the US government decided to defeat Cuba over the long term. To that end it established a complex package of sanctions and reprisals that were extended and reinforced by subsequent US administrations, the vital core of which remained the economic blockade and other measures to isolate Cuba from the rest of the world. With the collapse of socialism in Europe, the US thought that the time had come to give the final push to the Cuban revolution: a parallel to the 19th century when they described Cuba as a "ripe apple" waiting to drop into their hands.

As a consequence it did everything it could to precipitate the decomposition of our political-economic system and to defraud and divide the people. The economic blockade was intensified, first with the Torricelli Act (1992), which prevented US subsidiaries in third countries from trading with Cuba and imposed sanctions on vessels that docked in Cuban ports; and then with the Helms-Burton Act (1996), which took the economic siege to the highest level by sanctioning any foreign company trading with Cuba. At this time the United States also threatened to apply an article that allowed all Cuban Americans to file legal claims on their former properties, and formulated a program to reestablish neocolonial capitalism in our land. It created a subversive television channel and increased its radio transmissions to the island to 200 hours per day. It stimulated and backed terrorist groups within and outside the country and promoted an image of growing numbers of dissident factions. It compounded that by using the emigration issue (the rafters) as a means of destabilization, and by committing acts of biological warfare.

Why did the United States not change its policy of aggression toward Cuba, given that the "Soviet threat" had disappeared? The reason is evident. During the years of the Cold War, that was simply a pretext; the real US intention has always been to destroy the example of the island and to reincorporate Cuba as a US satellite.

What was Cuba's strategy under those circumstances of an unprecedented economic crisis and the brutal US offensive to destroy the revolution?

Cuba undertook its own unique route, based on the concept of preserving socialism in an even more Cuban form, by introducing various changes and reforms in an orderly way, without haste and in line with the exigencies of survival, and at the same time fighting external enemies on the essential ideological, political, economic and diplomatic planes.

The road to those reforms would not be without heartbreak and risks, but it was the only possible way to retain the achievements of the revolution and save socialism in its essential projection. No fanatical self-immolation and return to capitalism: Cuba sought an independent, original and well-considered solution in line with its needs. Thus the most profound and complex transformations since the radical structural changes of 1959–61 took place in Cuba.

Certain premises in those changes were decisive in preventing damage to the basic pillars of socialism. We resolved:

- Not to disregard the US threat and not to make any concessions to it.

- To build on the national unity of revolutionaries and patriots.

- To resist and not to abandon anyone or give up any of the revolution's principal social achievements.

- To identify errors, problems and deficiencies with the aim of overcoming them within socialism without becoming demoralized.

- To cherish and utilize the material and spiritual wealth created by the revolution.

- Not to isolate ourselves from the world: to accept the new international reality and operate within it.

- To guarantee increasing participation of the people in the exercise of revolutionary power by giving them more information without fearing constructive debate and the exercise of criticism.

- To be flexible in terms of responses and solutions without abandoning principles; to listen to and discuss foreign opinions, but to make our own decisions.

- To fortify the political role of the Cuban Communist Party (PCC) and the other popular revolutionary organizations.

- To evaluate, understand and avoid the errors that provoked the crisis and the defeat of "real socialism."

- To reemphasize the historical thread of the Cuban revolution, from José Martí to Fidel and Che.

From 1986 to mid-1989, Cubans lived through the process of "rectification of errors and negative tendencies," a fertile stage of search and debate on the best way forward for socialism. With the collapse of the East European regimes and then—in August 1991—of the Soviet Union, discussions on and interpretations of what had happened extended throughout the island. Moreover, questions and answers emerged about what to do in Cuba in order to preserve socialism, with a view to overcoming our own errors. The entire population—in every barrio, factory, office or school—became a parliament and discussion forum.

In May 1990 the fourth congress of the PCC was convened. A document was read and discussed by 3.5 million citizens, who made some 1.5 million recommendations and proposals that were collected in reports that served as a basis for the PCC congress.

Fidel inaugurated that congress and posed a central task: "Our most important duty is to analyze with a great deal of realism the current situation of our country, and to clearly comprehend that we are living in an exceptional period." He added: "The problem is… that what we have to do is save the homeland, the revolution and socialism in these exceptional circumstances." And he concluded: "The revolution has no alternative."

The congress reviewed the unique circumstances and adopted agreements and alignments that directed—in the new stage—the undertakings of the party and the whole society. Those agreements included important changes to the statutes and program of the

PCC, and to the state political system. At the same time, the congress approved an updated economic strategy for the "special period."

The congress advocated the strictest respect for internal debate, unity of action, and strict discipline and rigor in the fulfillment of party tasks. It insisted on the need for the party to listen and learn from the people, alongside its directional work. For the first time the PCC was defined as the "party of the Cuban nation"; in other words, of all Cubans and not of one particular class or sector. It admitted into its ranks any revolutionary religious believer who met the other membership requirements.

It recommended to the National Assembly that its members should be directly elected by popular vote, to fortify its strength and those of the provincial and municipal bodies of People's Power, and to guarantee a greater organized participation by citizens in the exercise of democracy. It reaffirmed that the party could not propose any People's Power candidate and that the latter had to be proposed by representatives of civil society organizations.

In his speech to the congress, Carlos Lage—a member of the Political Bureau—noted that in the face of the new world reality, the Cuban economy had to undergo a radical change and that this needed time.

A radical change and time to overcome the crisis, without being precise as to how much: two concepts defining the future awaiting the Cuban economy.

The PCC congress demonstrated that Cuba had correctly interpreted the magnitude of the crisis, and that it had the political and intellectual maturity and the moral reserve to defend its conquests, to resist, and to find solutions and move forward.

One consequence of the rapid and far-reaching events of 1989–91 was the need to modify the 1976 constitution and adapt it to the new national and international situation, and in the process, to improve some of its content and various formal and secondary aspects. In June 1992 the National Assembly approved a constitutional reform that covered 56 percent of the 1976 document, adding three new chapters and reducing it from 141 articles to 137. Of the remaining articles, 77 underwent some change. Those transformations summed up the wide-ranging democratic debate in civil society, and within the PCC and parliament, that had taken place since 1990.

The most notable changes to the constitution included the following:

- The regulatory framework was created to open up to foreign capital and to hand over property — except land — to workers' collectives on the large estates.
- National and provincial deputies were to be directly elected.
- The concept of the secular state was made more concrete.
- The PCC was defined as the vanguard of the Cuban nation.

Those constitutional reforms proved their worth in the following years, by allowing profound changes in the economic and political spheres without trauma or legal or doctrinal incoherence that might have put our stability at risk.

From 1961, and for more than 30 years, Cuba had not experienced the need to vary its economic structures. The reforms initiated in 1993 were unprecedented, as they arose from unique national and international circumstances.

The Cuban reforms did not come about through a movement or internal force pressuring for change, but were adopted and executed based on a consensus to save socialism rather than to facilitate a transition to capitalism. Of course, some of the reforms will bring new social contradictions, by generating illegitimate inequalities and possibly stimulating individualism and greed.

The danger of this should not be denied.

In less than four years, from 1993 to 1997, 19 economic reforms and other fundamental decisions expressed in law were adopted. For example, in 1993: the legalized use of foreign currency, the expansion of self-employment and the creation of the Basic Units of Cooperative Production in the agricultural sector. In 1994: the reorganization of the central state administration agencies, the cleansing of internal finances, the restructuring of prices and tariffs, the creation of a taxation system, the creation of farmers' markets and the industrial goods and craft markets, and the passing of the Mining Act. In 1995: authorization of a private restaurant market, the possibility of university professors entering the self-employed sector, and the passing of foreign investment legislation. In 1996: the creation of duty-free zones and industrial parks. In 1997: the founding of the Central Bank and regulation of banks and non-bank financial institutions. Other reforms included the decentralization and redirecting of foreign trade and various measures to improve productivity, efficiency and economic controls.

The question of whether the reforms were well directed can be answered by the fact that the economy halted its descent in 1994, grew by 2.5 percent in 1995, by 5 percent in 1996 and by more than 7 percent in 1997. The fiscal deficit went from 35 percent to less than 2.5 percent of GDP and the exchange rate for national currency decreased from 120–140 pesos down to 25 pesos per dollar. Foreign trade experienced a 30 percent recovery between 1995 and 1996. The number of joint ventures with foreign capital grew from 20 in 1990 to 300-plus. From 200,000 tourists in 1990 more than one million were scheduled to visit in 2005. Nickel production regained its 1989 level and production of oil doubled.

There are still many obstacles and problems to overcome. Without doubt, the US blockade is an enormous burden that prevents our more rapid advance, although a positive effect is that we have been obliged to seek a wider diversity of trade partners and investors, which affords our economy more flexibility and independence.

Internally, the reforms and other measures also brought negative effects in increased levels of social inequality compared to those prevailing up until 1989, and the emergence of issues that did not exist at that time such as prostitution in areas of tourism, corruption among certain low- and medium-level officials, and instances of drug abuse. That is why the battle against double standards, individualism and demoralization in the face of difficulties has become the primary struggle in overcoming the crisis in its essential political and ethical dimensions.

The support and moral and political reserves do exist to achieve success, although the battle will probably be longer and more complex than simply overcoming the economic aspect of the crisis. It demands more exemplary conduct from revolutionaries, more efficiency and better economic controls, improvements to the democratic participation of workers in making economic and political decisions in every workplace, and increased democratic participation of the people as a whole in the exercise of government.

Cuban foreign policy

Our foreign policy is formulated and carried out by a little country harassed by the mightiest power in the world. It is a simple policy based on the reality that the world has become globalized and dominated by one principal power — the United States — and a neoliberal hegemonic standard. Another consideration is the growing breach between the developed North and an increasingly impoverished South.

We also work on the basis of our conviction that the present world is not homogenous, and that the world never has been. It contains contradictions, cracks and spaces in which Cuba is seeking to survive, advance and gain time until the correlation of international forces changes. We are trying to contribute to that change in our daily undertakings, both within and outside of the island, in accordance with strict principles of respect for the self-determination and sovereignty of all nations and solidarity with all peoples and states.

We further believe that our major problems can only be solved to a limited extent in isolation within Cuba, as we are part of this planet and cannot marginalize ourselves from the global economic system and the irrational policy currently dominating it.

Thus we are constantly cooperating in the transformation of that system, in order to receive the benefits from a global order different from the present one: a multipolar order, with equitable economic relations and full respect for all states as equals. We are internationalists for ethical reasons, for strategic considerations and out of necessity. Throughout our history we have received solidarity at critical moments and thus we realize its importance for any nation.

Our first priority is to contribute to preserving the principles of international law, in which holes larger than the black holes of the universe have been opened, especially with regard to self-determination and sovereignty, to the solution of conflicts between countries by peaceful means, to respect for equality among states. In the final analysis, the precepts of the United Nations inscribed in its charter are being ignored and trampled over by the United States and the other great powers that control the UN Security Council, the International Monetary Fund and other major international bodies.

We are also untiring fighters against unequal terms of exchange and foreign debt, which are increasingly asphyxiating two thirds of the nations of the world. We criticize non-tariff protectionism.

"Yes," say the governments of the North, "we are going to eliminate trade barriers, we are going to unite markets," but they continue to maintain and reinforce the invisible threads that benefit their products to the detriment of ours. They affirm that borders are to disappear, but the interests of the great powers have not been extinguished. Moreover, we are waging a fierce struggle against US privileges in the United Nations. We are working toward the expansion of the Security Council to include many other countries, such as Brazil and India. How can it be that Latin America and the Caribbean, with a collective population of 450 million people, do not have a permanent member on the Security Council? We advocate the democratization of international relations and this includes various economic and diplomatic issues.

Obviously, it is a concrete priority for our nation to defeat the blockade on our country imposed by the United States nearly 40 years ago. The blockade prevents us from importing even a single aspirin from that country, and backed by the Helms-Burton Act, the United States is pursuing any businessperson who comes to do business with Cuba. A terrible and anachronistic fact, but that is how it is: if a piece of equipment—acquired for example from a German company that has merged with a US one—breaks down in a hospital, we are simply unable to buy the necessary spare parts. The blockade is brutal and criminal. The international community has overwhelmingly rejected it every year since 1992 in the United Nations, but the United States pays no attention and persists in persecuting Cuba. It believes that it is the sheriff of the world and maintains its siege against all costs. This aggressive and arrogant policy is already morally defeated and our country will not rest until it is totally abandoned—without concessions on our part, since we have never done anything to provide a basis for those sanctions, which are unprecedented in the history of humanity.

We are not going to relinquish our right to do freely in Cuba what we as Cubans want. Moreover, we have the means to defend ourselves: a people armed, trained and aware, united and prepared to fight for the liberty of our homeland and the social system that we have democratically elected.

We do not want war; on the contrary, we are a peaceful people. We have always been disposed to negotiate our differences with the United States, but on an equal footing, with mutual respect and without conditions on either side.

It is a fact that very complex issues exist. If the United States had acted with more foresight, it would have already received compensation for the monopolies and enterprises Cuba confiscated from 1959 to 1961. But instead of negotiation it wanted to destroy us, and the damage it has caused now amounts to far more than the value of those properties. It is the United States that is indebted to Cuba, and this is regrettable, because the deaths, injuries, unnecessary costs and material destruction wreaked on the island are incommensurable and irreparable. The Spanish got their compensation, the British got theirs, but "Hey!" said the US aggressors, "We are going to crush them!" So we had the Bay of Pigs in 1961, economic warfare, terrorism, sabotage, biological and psychological warfare, assassination attempts on Fidel, and actions to isolate us. Despite all this, we have no animosity towards the people of the United States. On the contrary, in Cuba we admire their virtues and nobility. We keep up to date with the best US films on television and in the movie theaters — free, since we copy them: the blockade has some advantages. Our youth enjoy rock music, as well as our *son*; the Cuban people appreciate US culture and can differentiate between the pseudo-cultural trash and dregs of that society and the grandeur of its artists, intellectuals, scientists, philosophers and decent citizens.

The struggle between Cuba and the United States has been compared to that between David and Goliath. We have grown stronger and more intelligent, and in the end, invincible, thanks to our giant enemy.

It is indispensable for Cuba not to be isolated from the world. At present, we have relations with more than 160 nations, and close to 90 embassies. When the Pope said that Cuba should open itself up to the world, we had been open to it since 1959; that is true in the context of our identity and respect for those who respect us. In any event, we were grateful for that remark, as the Pope also added: "and let the world open up to Cuba." Every year we welcome dozens of presidents, foreign ministers and leaders from all over the world. Cuba is a venue for various international events, including summits of heads of state and government; and on this continent, we participate in the Ibero-American summits, the Association of Caribbean States and the Latin American Economic System. We have a clear profile in the United Nations. We are founding members of the Movement of Nonaligned Countries and the Group of 77.

Naturally, Cuba's priority is Latin America and the Caribbean. We advocate cooperation and the integration of all the countries we consider sister nations. And we reject US pretensions to definitively convert those countries into a dependent market through the FTAA. Cooperation between nations—alongside fundamental changes within many of them, to be decided independently by each nation—is the only way to achieve sustainable development, social justice, and genuine self-determination and sovereignty. The US plan, on the other hand, would lead to the destruction of the freedom of nations, to their domination by a single power, and more underdevelopment, polarization and injustice.

Venezuela occupies an outstanding place in our relations with the region. Since our relations with Venezuela were restored in 1989, first under the government of Carlos Andrés Pérez and subsequently under that of Rafael Caldera, the trend has been towards increased cultural relations and diplomatic, scientific and sporting exchanges, and increased trade with Venezuelan companies. That has given rise to a bilateral chamber of commerce, a parliamentary friendship group, and certain joint actions on the part of state institutions and civil society in the two countries. Now, of course, it is becoming all the more necessary to convert those formal agreements into tangible facts.

I conclude with Martí: "Homeland is humanity!" Cuban foreign policy will always seek to serve humanity and not to isolate Cuba from any collective action. It will be the consistent expression of our constitutional guidelines, founded on another of Martí's precepts: "I would wish that the first law of our Republic should be Cuba's support for the full dignity of all peoples."

Cooperation between Cuba and Venezuela

Questions and answers at Venezuela's National Defense Studies Institute, 2002.

Question: How many Cuban doctors and sports instructors are there in Venezuela, what benefits do they receive from the Venezuelan government, and how are they paid?

Germán Sánchez: I should explain that there is an Integral Co-operation Agreement between Cuba and Venezuela covering the presence here of sports instructors, doctors and other specialists, signed by the two presidents on October 30, 2000. That agreement has two parts: the first part being virtually the same as the energy agreement that the government of Venezuela signed one week previously with a group of Caribbean and Central American countries.

Within that agreement the beneficiary countries, including Cuba, can buy oil at world market prices, but with one benefit. Based on the average annual price per barrel, Venezuela will make a loan to the countries benefiting from this agreement, fluctuating between 5 and 25 percent. This Caracas Energy Agreement is the first part of the Integral Cooperation Agreement between Cuba and Venezuela, through which Cuba benefits in the same way as the other countries in the region.

The Integral Cooperation Agreement has another aspect whereby primarily Venezuela receives the benefits, although it also favors Cuba. The agreement draws on the strengths in our country that Venezuela can utilize in line with its own interests. In the field of public health, our country has made internationally acknowledged advances, including in preventive medical care. Likewise, in terms of medical developments, Cuba is highly advanced in applied biotechnology and biogenetics, particularly in the field of human health, including in vaccines obtained through recombinative methods and other similar discoveries. Cuba also manufactures and exports hi-tech medical equipment. Thus, in the field of public health Venezuela has much to utilize from Cuba.

As you know, our country is strong in sports: with 11 million inhabitants and 11 gold medals in the last Olympic Games, we won the largest number of gold medals per capita, more than the United States, more than any other nation. Those gold medals are the fruit of a 40-year-old policy of developing sports, physical education and recreation among the population almost from birth. This is something else to be utilized by Venezuela.

Then there is the sugar industry, where Cuban capacity and experience can be shared with Venezuela, which used to produce sugar to meet its own needs but some years back became a net importer of sugar. Venezuela has better climatic conditions and soil than Cuba for cultivating excellent cane sugar, as well as the personnel, the capital and the workforce to produce harvests that could lead to self-sufficiency in this crop and even the export of sugar and its by-products.

Cuba is an island with an exceptional sugar tradition dating back to the beginning of the 19th century, and we have been an exporter of other sugarcane by-products for the last 40 years.

Although alcohol and rum are always highlighted, there are many other products: wood, paper, fertilizer, electrical energy, animal feed; sugar cane has great potential in all these products and Cuba has made significant advances in that context. Technical advice from Cuba can help Venezuela reactivate and develop its sugar and sugar by-products industry. For example, the first request made to us was to contribute to the updating and restoration of the former Tocuyo sugar refinery, now called Pío Tamayo. In just four or five months, Cuban and Venezuelan technical personnel and Venezuelan workers had made operational a refinery that had been paralyzed for two years. The refinery is about to mill its first harvest.

Our experience in education and teaching people to read and write can also be utilized by Venezuela. Literacy is a fundamental aspect of any country's development, whether it is capitalist or otherwise. There is a basic principle: people who cannot read or write are unable to fulfill their duties or their rights as citizens in a complete sense. Moreover, from a humanitarian, social and economic point of view it is indispensable for the inhabitants of any country to know how to read and write, and to be educated at least to intermediate grade. Without that, economic development is impossible. Cuba eradicated illiteracy more than 40 years ago, in 1961: an experience studied by specialists from various countries which can also aid Venezuela.

As far as adult education is concerned, after the literacy campaign we developed campaigns for adults to reach sixth and ninth grades. Currently, our average education level extends to the second and third year of high school, and is the highest in Latin America.

Today Cuba has an education system that is totally free from infant day care until postgraduate studies, and free to everyone, whoever they might be, without discrimination of any kind. The education system includes programs of special education, rural education, different specialties at university level, and more recently, the use of educational television and new educational concepts in elementary, secondary and university teaching.

So how many Cuban doctors and sports instructors are in Venezuela and under what conditions? This is a subject on which there has been much speculation and an enormous number of lies. At the end of 1999 a group of 454 doctors, nurses and health technicians arrived in Venezuela in the wake of the Vargas [land-slide] disaster. As circumstances gradually normalized, those doctors returned to Cuba; however, given the health care needs of the population of Vargas, which were not covered by other Venezuelan specialists, it was decided that around 100 of those Cuban volunteers would stay on until December 2000. Then what happened? Other Venezuelan communities, through their governors, mayors and representatives, realized that these doctors could be very useful in remote settlements where no medical attention was available, or where there were outpatient depart-ments without doctors.

A request went out for doctors for those places. In that context there are currently 280 doctors and a number of nurses in nine Venezuelan states. Under what conditions? First, Cuba does not consider whether the political position of a mayor or governor is x, y or z, it merely evaluates the request for humanitarian aid and the needs of the population, and then contributes in whatever way possible. Second, our doctors are not contracted in the sense that they receive a salary. Cuba continues to pay their wages, their families continue to receive their salary in full. Venezuela only as-sumes responsibility for their board and lodging (although many of them live in outpatient departments), and a sum of money for food, internal transportation costs and phone calls: in other words, their food plus the equivalent of $100 per month for those expenses.

I would like to say that medical collaboration with other

countries is not a new Cuban policy. For our population, we have the largest number of doctors in the world. In Cuba there is one doctor for every 160 inhabitants and we have a network of medical facilities based on the basic unit of the family doctor; that means that all Cuban families, wherever they live — in the city, the country or in the mountains — are under the constant care of a doctor and a nurse. That is the starting point of our health system, and then there are the polyclinics and the specialized hospitals. The family doctors are themselves specialists, not young people who have just graduated, but physicians who have continued training until they are general physicians. Those doctors are experienced in gynecology, pediatrics, and are capable of giving follow-up treatment at home to post-operative cases; moreover, they know the old man of 70 and go to take his blood pressure every day if necessary. Nurses have a monitoring role: with diabetics and with the program of vaccinations for children from birth onwards. Cuba has had a triple vaccination program for many years now. Cuba was the first Latin American country to eradicate poliomyelitis in the 1960s, and Cuban scientists have discovered a vaccine against meningitis and are currently working on others, including against AIDS and cholera.

Our doctors are trained to serve the people, not to take advantage of them or to treat them like "clients." For 40 years generations of our doctors have assimilated a humanitarian ethic of solidarity. And, as part of their training, in order to make them even more capable of comprehending the grandeur of their profession, those who wish to travel to foreign countries under certain voluntary conditions can do so. The overwhelming majority are prepared to do that. One of the aspirations of our medical students is to go to an African or Latin American country. Those values have been encouraged, based on the teachings of Martí and Bolívar, as well as the socialist and Christian principle of serving one's neighbor. It might seem strange and hard to understand, but here in Venezuela we have the experience and the positive feedback of Venezuelan men and women who have been treated by our doctors. For 40 years, and particularly in the last 30 years, between 35,000 and 40,000 doctors have traveled to more than 60 countries on this kind of humanitarian mission. Currently, there are 400 Cuban doctors in Guatemala. There are more Cuban doctors in Guatemala than in Venezuela and the government of Guatemala has voted against Cuba for two successive years at the Human Rights Commission in Geneva, under pressure from the United States as part of the maneuver it engages in every year as a way of justifying the blockade.

In Haiti, one of the most backward countries in the world, on a par with the poorest countries in Africa, there are more than 400 Cuban doctors. In Haiti there are more Cuban doctors than Haitian doctors working within the state health system. They have therefore become a basic element in the health care of that backward and impoverished country.

Cuban doctors are in Africa, Brazil and Paraguay. Our doctors are not present only in countries that have an allied or friendly government to Cuba.

In the case of sports instructors, this is a technical service that Venezuela pays for as it did during the period of Carlos Andrés Pérez and Caldera: we have more than 2,000 Cuban sports instructors—some of them in European nations—offering a specialized technical service, just like trainers from the United States, Russia and other countries, and they are paid for their services. But with the characteristic, of course, that our prices are way below the international level and our sports instructors in Venezuela are also people who, above all, have come here to help, not to make money. They have come to fulfill a mission of solidarity, and work with an exceptional love so that Venezuela can develop into an athletic power in Latin America.

During the [attempted] coup d'état [against President Chávez] in April 2002 and the repression that was unleashed in those bitter 48 hours, when some of our compañeros were raided, pushed around, and had their houses searched for weapons, we decided to evacuate the sports instructors. They gathered at various points and the planes were already revving their engines in Cuba, when on Saturday April 13 the situation began to change and our decision was reversed. At the time, many Venezuelans living in the 22 states where our sports and physical education instructors are located broke down in tears and embraced the Cubans. They were their pupils, families of their pupils and friends who spontaneously testified for them: it was a profound and sentimental moment. In barely 12 months of the instructors' presence here, the grateful and noble Venezuelan people knew the nature of those men and women whom they were bidding farewell, and who were all leaving with just one suitcase. They had to leave many of their belongings behind because they couldn't be transported on the plane. "Don't worry, we'll look after them for you," "You can trust us," said the Venezuelans, in a moving expression of fraternity.

Those athletes are in 22 states and 140 municipalities run by governors and mayors of all political tendencies. In this context, politics does not exist: there is no political training here as claimed by those loudmouthed instigators of destabilization and fascism. On the contrary, on leaving Havana they were all instructed not to get involved in Venezuelan politics. They talk about Cuba, but not about Venezuela, although they might have their views. In part, this is to avoid manipulation, but above all, it is based on a fundamental principle: they came here to aid development in physical education and health, not to transmit some kind of ideology. It is not our place to do so, that is an issue for Venezuelans.

In addition to the sports instructors there is the group of sugar technicians and another group working to set up a sugar and sugar by-products agribusiness complex in Barinas. Other Cuban specialists in education, culture and tourism are also working here on short-term contracts.

Part of the agreement includes a Cuban commitment to give free medical treatment to poor and sick Venezuelans. That program has been misrepresented; it involves medical attention in Cuba when the patients are suffering from complex illnesses. Obviously people with a cold aren't sent to Cuba, but only people with difficult diseases, some incurable in Venezuela and others that are curable but very costly. We give patients free treatment and the Venezuelan government covers their flights to Cuba.

Cuban socialism and Chinese socialism

Question: From the 1960s the People's Republic of China has been moving towards socialism with the characteristics of a very pragmatic capitalism, within what they call socialism "the Chinese way." What do you think of this Chinese development and what have been the principal similarities and differences with regard to the future of Cuba?

Germán Sánchez: We are fanatical defenders of every country's self-determination and sovereignty. We are also respectful of the concept that every country has the right to freely elect the socialist process—if that is what it has chosen—that best approximates its realities. It is not possible to compare a country with a culture like Cuba's, which is Western, rational and Christian in its roots, with a country like China, which has such a distinctive culture. China is a country with more than one billion inhabitants, or 100 times the population of Cuba. And, I believe that China is more than 12,000 kilometers from the United States, whilst we feel the US breathing down our necks every morning. It is said that in Cuba we have no opposition; but we have the greatest opposition that any government could have. From the United States we are bombarded daily with hundreds of hours of subversive radio, not to mention a TV channel that they have the nerve to name after José Martí, which cannot be seen thanks to our technicians. It is neither seen nor heard, but is nevertheless subsidized by the US government.

The Chinese experience is extremely interesting. We have sent people to China in order to learn about it, because we want to assimilate what might be of relevance to Cuba. Cuba is an open country. Instead of retreating from the world, we feel very close to all the nations of the planet, to all cultures. Cubans are noted for their universal vision and this history is facilitated by the island's geographical position: we were always linked to the outside world. And thus we are aware of China's political and economic experiences: specialists in economics and political leaders go there, we have academics studying China, and there are many exchanges. We act in the same way with the United States, Europe, Africa and our own region. That includes specialists belonging to the Rockefeller group and friends of the United States who have been to Cuba, or who have been unable to travel to Cuba but have met our people in Mexico, and who were studying that country's management techniques. We are not going to the United States anymore because we have been banned, but we would be delighted to know of all that country's advances. They are the ones who don't want exchanges.

We have a relationship of understanding with China, of agreement on a series of problems facing the world today. China has a concept of market socialism, in line with its realities: we do not criticize them, they are advancing, they have problems from the ethical point of view, for example, large-scale corruption; but China emerged from a situation of extreme poverty to become a world power and there are noteworthy nutritional, technological, scientific, professional and educational developments in China.

These achievements were born of a socialism with its own particular characteristics: for example, the socialism that they refer to as market socialism, where the market operates within its own laws.

For us the market in Cuban socialism is a reality that cannot be avoided, but we cannot submit ourselves to the market, to the rules of the market. And in order to differentiate our socialism from that of China, which is "market socialism," as they have theorized it, ours is "socialism with a market." We accept the market, but we accept it reluctantly. We rejected it to a large extent based on certain concepts of the law of value in the 1960s, 1970s and 1980s. Later, we had to undertake a series of reforms and understand that the world had changed, and we had to adjust ourselves to the new realities. In the 1990s Cuba was the country that undertook the most reforms in the world, except of course the countries that collapsed; in those cases they were not reforms anyway, because reforms are about changes that don't alter the nature of the system, or its principal features. The collapse of the Soviet Union was a reversion to capitalism.

We transformed socialism in Cuba and adapted it to the new realities. We understood that we had committed certain errors, but we preserved the essential aspects. We realized that we had to develop various markets: for example, the new free farmers' markets were based on the principle of equality as far as possible, of distributing what we had among everyone. And now we have free farmers' markets, free craft markets, free industrial markets, we even have a market in foreign currency, in which more than one billion dollars are collected per annum. Why did we do that? Because we decided not to hand over the private market to transnational capital. Those transnationals turned up when we started to undertake the reforms: McDonald's and the other US chains. Instead of McDonald's we introduced Burgui, and made better hamburgers than McDonald's, and we began to manufacture our own soft drinks. We imported Coca-Cola because some tourists like it, but we produced Tropi-Cola, which is really tasty, and we have competitive and delicious brands of beer, made in Cuba. In this way, close to 70 percent of tourist consumption in Cuba is of Cuban-manufactured products. When tourism first took off we had no choice and 80 percent of what was consumed was imported, because we were in crisis. We solved that with a sustained policy of stimulating national production for tourism. There are many things that are characteristic of Cuban socialism, just as Chinese socialism has its own characteristics. We respect that experience, they respect us and we are firm friends.

Cuba and the US blockade

Question: According to the treatment of Cuba under the Helms-Burton Act, ships docking at the island cannot subsequently dock at US ports for a period of six months. How have you been able to overcome that restriction and how has it influenced the island's commercial and tourist development? Also, how are the Cuban people preparing for the historic visit that you are soon to receive from ex-US President Jimmy Carter?

Germán Sánchez: Visits to Cuba by public figures always arouse global interest. When the Pope visited Cuba, it provoked a huge media campaign. I was in Caracas at the time. It was being said that the Pope had brought down socialism in Poland, and so they affirmed: "Now it's Cuba's turn." Never had so many journalists arrived in Cuba. That was four years ago and both Cuban socialism and the Pope still exist. We have received such visitors for years from all over the world and we set no limits: on the contrary, we are happy for people of all persuasions to come to Cuba, with the exception of terrorists and fascists, of course. We are very happy that they should learn something of the Cuban experience, and for us to learn a few things too, even from the enemy. We have learnt a lot from foreigners by talking with them.

The Helms-Burton Act is the consolidation and apex of the blockade that the United States imposed in the early years of the 1960s, when the US government did not accept the revolution, whether socialist or otherwise. At that time we were not socialists but simply nationalists of a popular orientation, and we passed an agrarian reform act that affected US interests, because US companies owned hundreds of thousands of hectares of idle land. Justice was done and that provoked a spiral of confrontations during which Cuba decided that socialism was the only way to achieve genuine independence, development, democracy and social justice for the overwhelming majority of the people. At that point the United States began to try to asphyxiate us with an economic blockade. In the early stages, given that the Soviet Union replaced to a large extent the economic links that had existed with our neighbor, we transformed our economy and the effects of the blockade were alleviated to a certain extent.

Another current emerged in the United States that argued that it was better to solve the Cuban conflict through rapprochement and constructive relations. After many years of confrontation, they have managed to solve the problem with Vietnam, and with China, so they say, "Why not with Cuba?" This argument is steadily gaining ground in the United States among Republicans, Democrats, and public opinion generally, which is much more important. During the Carter government it was decided to create the Interests Section: not an embassy, but a diplomatic representation in Havana and another in Washington. That facilitates dialogue on any dangerous situation. At that time, Carter also authorized subsidiaries of US transnationals to trade with Cuba, subsidiaries located in Mexico and Venezuela, and in that way US transnationals could sell us their goods. This was very positive for us and for them as well. We reached the point of buying up to

$500 million worth of goods every year.

Then came Reagan and Bush and we were demonized once again, and the collapse of our Eastern European allies and the Soviet Union occurred. Because they believed that Cuba was a satellite of the Soviet Union, according to the law of gravity, they thought if the planet that was the Soviet Union fell, so would its tiny satellite. That is what they believed in the early 1990s, that a puff of wind would be enough to topple us. The theory of the "ripe apple," prevalent in the United States in the 19th century, was revived. At the end of that century, when Cuba had already defeated Spain, the United States intervened, believing Cuba to be "ripe for the taking." A US vessel (the *Maine*) was blown up in the Bay of Havana. Although it is still not known if the United States itself was responsible, that was the pretext to intervene: Spain had been defeated by our people, blow by blow, militarily, popularly, and yet victory was snatched from us by the United States.

When the Soviet Union collapsed, they thought that once again the moment had arrived to devour the "ripe fruit," and launched a new attack. First it was the Torricelli Act, which essentially banned US transnationals in third countries from trading with us, and also included a measure concerning shipping. But they weren't satisfied, because the Cuban mafia in Miami has a lot of power. They are terrorists, *mafiosi* who have their tentacles reaching into Congress and who have direct connections with some presidents—like the present one [George W. Bush], whom in fact they enthroned through electoral fraud. So they said: "Soon we are going to take over the island again, fire on Cuba!" Then the pirate aircraft and terrorists began to fly over Havana. Imagine that suddenly aircraft belonging to Colombian paramilitaries begin to arrive and drop here—over Caracas—flyers, and this happens once, twice, three times, even after they are given more than 20 warnings. President Clinton verbally committed himself through an intermediary to prevent further flights, and simply failed to fulfill that promise. Once again, they crossed the border, and unfortunately, they had to be brought down.

This became the pretext for passing the Helms-Burton bill that was already being debated, and they decided to fast track the decision. Within three days, it was passed. The Helms-Burton Act represented a detailed codification of the blockade, the longest lasting in history, against a small and peaceful country that tried only to advance its society in a just and equitable manner.

In the face of that, what could we do? When the act began to be applied, in March 1996, some businesspeople who were negotiating with us got scared, because they faced being banned from entering the United States under the infamous Title III, which threatened seizure of their properties in the United States if they bought former US properties in Cuba. Then they did something incredible: it was no longer just the properties of US entrepreneurs that we had nationalized in the 1960s that were included under the Helms-Burton Act, but also the properties of Cubans who had subsequently become US citizens. Well, the legislation was financed by Bacardi and by the Cuban American National Foundation (CANF); they got what they wanted, of course.

Some enterprises felt inhibited, but many others continued doing business with Cuba, sometimes with some highly original legal formulas. The law damaged us, for example, by banning ships from entering US ports for six months after docking in Cuba. What did that signify in practical terms? The ships kept arriving, but we had to pay them more, the fleets charged us more for damages and prejudice. Nevertheless, the boats kept coming to Cuba.

Despite the Helms-Burton Act, we began to recover. The economy declined like a war economy between 1991 and 1994 and GDP dropped by 34 percent. It was a war without bullets. Then, from 1995, after the reforms of 1993–94, we began to recover, and in the last five years of the decade Cuba had the highest economic growth in Latin America. In the last five years of the 1990s our GDP grew in excess of 4.6 percent and that of Latin America grew by 3.2 percent. Here we are not talking about per capita growth, because the Cuban population is barely increasing and that of Latin America is increasing rapidly. In other words, the per capita rate is very much in favor of Cuba.

And so, despite the Helms-Burton Act, the Cuban economy continued to prosper, achieving more efficiency and improved productivity through the application of modern techniques and methods in the direction of the economy. Of course, we are still in a situation where there are problems and inefficiencies. For example, in oil: because we received oil from the Soviet Union at a very reasonable price in exchange for sugar, little effort was made in that sector and we continued using Soviet techniques and backward technology. Now, things have radically changed through the opening up of the oil market to prospecting. We divided all of our geological areas into blocks and foreign oil companies began to arrive—but not US companies, which are prohibited by their own nation's laws. This year Cuba is set to produce almost 50 percent of the oil it consumes, and within our development prospects, based on proven reserves of oil with a high sulfur content, we have acquired the techniques to generate electricity. Thermoelectric stations have been adapted to burn national crude, thanks to a series of investments, and the accompanying natural gas is already being used with a cutting-edge combined-cycle technology, thus providing us with cheap electricity.

At the end of the day, maybe we'll be grateful to those myopic US administrations, which have done us the favor of forcing Cuba to become one of the countries with the most balanced economic relations in Latin America and the world. José Martí taught us: "The nation that buys, rules." That is more complex in today's world. Cuba has relations with Europe, Latin America, Canada, China, Japan and Africa. We have diplomatic links with more than

170 countries and more than 100 embassies. We have commercial relations with more than 3,000 enterprises throughout the world and we owe that to the United States, because the blockade has obliged us to scratch around here and scratch around there, to decide that if rice is sold more cheaply in Indonesia, we'll go to find rice there. The United States has obliged us to be more independent, and that is one of the concerns of the US business sector.

Once again, there is the example of oil. What we have at the moment are some oilfields between Havana and Matanzas where oil is extracted along the coast, as there are several shallow underwater deposits. But at sea, Cuba has the area of its own landmass of 110,000 kilometers in the Gulf of Mexico, which belongs to us according to the law of the sea. In one third of the Gulf, in the Mexican area, there is oil; in the other third, belonging to the United States, there is oil. The remaining third is Cuban and we would have to be supremely unlucky if there was no oil in our section, where preliminary geological studies reveal very interesting zones. Why were they not explored before? In our case, we did not have the technology needed for the depths of those maritime zones. Now we do have the technology, and moreover, it is economically viable. So what did we do last year? We opened up the Gulf of Mexico. Repsol, a Spanish company, should sink the first well next year. What is the reaction of the US oil companies? They are concerned, because they are being left out. When the blockade is lifted and they can come in, many of those sites will probably already be controlled, under contracts exceptionally advantageous for us. This is one example of how we have developed our economy and our strategies under the relentless blockade.

There has been a recent experience with the United States at the time of Hurricane Michelle. Last year, after multiple discussions, they decided to allow the export of medicines and food — although without any financing, which is a highly limiting factor, and based on a series of requirements that made the operation very difficult. We said "No, with those conditions, we aren't interested: but if you set it up with financing and with the possibility of us also being able to sell, or at least with financing, let's see how it goes." The hurricane happened, and they sent a note that was a genuine gesture, stating that they were disposed to help with medicines and foodstuffs—but we replied in the negative. We didn't want gifts, what we wanted was to replace the reserves that we had to invest in foodstuffs and certain medicines. And they replied: "All right." This was an interesting experience, because it was confirmed that Cuba can be an important purchaser of foodstuffs, medicines and other goods from that country, and US businesspeople demonstrated that they are good at their job. An excellent relationship was immediately formed: we bought frozen chicken, some grains, and the appetite of the business sector was whetted. There are governors behind this sector who have visited Cuba.

The governor of Illinois was in Cuba more or less at the same time as Chávez in 1999. In similar statements to Chávez, the governor of Illinois, a Republican, acknowledged Cuba's advances on issues that many people highlight, but which coming from a Republican governor sounded more scandalous. Recently, US university students have arrived in ships and have met with our students and toured the capital.

Similarly, many US tourists travel to the island in violation of the blockade and the laws of the United States. The citizens of the most "free" country in the world cannot travel 150 kilometers to the south without risking a prison term of at least two years and fines of up to $20,000. Well, the forbidden fruit is to everybody's liking. We got around that—the prohibition—and thus, last year, more than 80,000 US citizens traveled to Cuba. How strange: they come through Cancún or other places, and when they get to Cuba, the "totalitarian" country where they are told there is no liberty, they are welcomed with smiles and can move about freely

24 hours a day, anywhere. Their passports are not even stamped, because if we were to do that they might have problems. They arrive at the airport, they are surprised and comment: "Hey, an airport, there are lights, how pretty, that's great, there are people in the street, people are dressed, there are no beggars, no children asking for money, no street kids."

They don't see any, because there aren't any. They begin to get curious and discover that they can hire a car or take a taxi and ask: "Can you take me to a house that someone will rent to me?" and the taxi driver says: "Sure." They find out that they can tour the country. Even better, that way they spend more. As you can imagine, no system of police supervision is capable of pursuing 80,000 gringos or the close to two million tourists that came to the island last year.

That is the situation. In reality, the blockade has been defeated. It is being maintained artificially. Carter's visit is very important because he was the president who held that view. We are preparing to receive him or any other visitor. Our people are educated, political, informed and welcoming.

We are currently experiencing a new stage in the education and information revolution. In the midst of all these circumstances provoked by the Helms-Burton Act, this year a program was instigated to guarantee pupils in the elementary grades one television per classroom, not for watching cartoons, but for educational programs that complement the work of classroom teachers. It is going to be extended to the entire country: one teacher and television for every 20 elementary schoolchildren.

We have launched a channel exclusively dedicated to education. For more than 12 months courses have been offered by television in English, French, art appreciation, Cuban history, world history, Latin American history, Spanish grammar and computing. In other words, Cuba is living through a flourishing phase from the educational and cultural point of view: we are establishing colleges for the training of art instructors — we have many, but in Cuba, as in Venezuela, there is infinite talent. We are ensuring that every child has access to an instructor. It is a whole concept of universalizing education and culture to an even greater degree, which is definitely the raison d'être of a genuine revolution: to make people more content, cultured, educated and informed of what is happening in the world.

The people of Cuba experienced the recent events in April [the attempted coup against President Hugo Chávez] alongside the people of Venezuela. On Saturday April 13, when Television Venezolana began to operate, it was transmitted live, and nobody in Cuba went to bed until Chávez had returned. Here at the Cuban embassy, we were besieged and attacked, and despite the fact that I invited in two television channels, no channel transmitted anything that I said. I don't know what happened to freedom of speech, to democracy, but we were attacked and almost killed, and the press censored us. We were discriminated against and silenced by the Venezuelan press in such dramatic circumstances, where there was the risk of a horrendous crime. This has left an indelible stain on the Venezuelan press.

Cuban television has lots of public affairs programs on international and national issues. People are very well informed as to what is happening in the world. That is one of the reasons that we are able to talk to God and the devil and their intermediaries who come to the island without any kind of complex, looking people in the eye with the respect that they merit in line with their respect for us.

3. In the line of fire

In your pages there will be no passion other than that for justice,
nor pen other than for those who move it with honor.

—José Martí

Permission to express an opinion on Cuba
(Letter to *El Nacional*, March 11, 2000)

Cuba is the subject of the most diverse opinions in the Venezuelan press. After a speech given by President Hugo Chávez in the University of Havana last November, the issue took on an exceptional intensity.

In Havana, Chávez had said:

> I have not the slightest doubt that the course being constructed by the mobilized Venezuelan people, on the very crest of the wave, is the same course, is combined with and going in the same direction, toward the same sea to which the Cuban people are marching. And beyond Cuba and Venezuela, I have no doubt that the peoples throughout Latin America and the Caribbean, little by little, some first and others later, will be taking a similar course toward a sea of happiness, of genuine human justice, of genuine peace, of genuine dignity.

Any unbiased interpretation would conclude that Chávez was

not talking about copying the Cuban social system, or saying that Cuba is a "sea of happiness." He even stated that our processes should each have their own spirit, their own essence.

A few days later, in a press conference on the subject, Fidel Castro reaffirmed the originality of our processes. As he explained:

> The bases of our constitutions have core differences: for example, in respect to the economic and social system of owner-ship; while the similarities are those that are found in all the constitutions in the world.
>
> I have never heard one single word from President Chávez about establishing socialism in Venezuela, although his op-position to neoliberalism is evident.
>
> Chávez's political ideas are rooted in the history of Venezuela, and essentially, in those of Simón Bolívar.

Previously, at the Central University of Venezuela on February 3, 1999, Fidel had stated: "Not even a revolution like ours... could have resisted; we could not have preserved the revolution in the current circumstances of this globalized world." Thus, Fidel did not come to encourage any imitation of Cuba. But he did emphasize that he saw "an exceptional hope for Venezuela in the hopes of this people."

Some people are committing the error of claiming that the Cuban economy is a disaster. Last year Cuba grew by 6.2 percent while the rest of Latin America and the Caribbean grew by barely 0.2 percent. From 1995 to 1999, Cuba's GDP increased, on average, by 3.6 percent, and that of the region by just 3.2 percent.

After the acute crisis from 1991 to 1994, the Cuban economy began a sustained recovery and almost all the world's experts agree that it will continue to advance successfully.

Our detractors refer to "the Cuban dictatorship," echoing that "Made in the USA" slogan to confuse the unsuspecting. The laws and decisions of the Cuban state are based on a popular consensus, without which it would have been impossible to maintain our social system under the ferocious attack of the United States. One may disagree with our political system, but nobody can deny that Cuban society is governed by constitutional norms and legitimate laws and institutions — adopted in a sovereign and democratic manner by Cubans — which should be respected.

Other people allege that Venezuela is conceding handouts to Cuba. It is totally false to say that the decision to increase economic and commercial relations between the two countries presupposes that Venezuela has given something to Cuba or is involved in exchanges or businesses that are affecting its interests, in the oil sector or any other sector.

Our links have been fruitful in the last 10 years. Important intergovernmental agreements have been signed to facilitate the current advances. Trade has been in excess of $400 million since 1996. Venezuela has been Cuba's largest trade partner in the region and its prime supplier of oil and its derivatives for some years.

Cuba is becoming steadily more attractive to foreign capital. In barely 10 years, 370 associations with foreign capital from Canada, Spain, France, Mexico, Israel, China, Italy and other countries have been established. Venezuela has the enormous advantage of proximity and common identity. The increase in trade between the two countries is taking place due to the economic "law of gravity," which functions best when sovereignty prevails.

Notorious enemies of the Cuban revolution are always repeating their slanders against our country. What is surprising are the statements and incorrect allusions by certain people who, up until recently, maintained close ties of friendship and solidarity with Cuba. There are even some who are attempting to resuscitate the nightmare of the Cold War and McCarthy-style anticommunism.

Everyone should be allowed to think as they wish. I only ask for respect for my people, who are striving with dignity, sacrifice and humanity to advance a social project that—like any earthly task—has its imperfections, but which represents the zenith of human achievement and a viable and irreversible development alternative for Cuba.

The Venezuelan people are the masters of their own destiny. This was confirmed in the article by Freddy Yépez, "Up to what point is Fidel guilty?" in which he proposes: "Instead of living by falsifying realities and blaming Fidel Castro for our problems, let us find our own ways of solving them."

Those people who, in the fervor of an electoral campaign, are taking up the attacks on Cuba as their banner, are diverting the central debate, which concerns the realities of their own country. We will never involve ourselves in this internal dispute. The people of Venezuela will elect their president, not the Cubans. And we, of course, will respect the sovereign will of this sister people.

We are not attempting to export the Cuban revolution (Interview with *Excelencia* magazine, September 2000)

Introduction: There are diplomats who carry out their mission without attracting attention. But there are also those who are condemned to the "eye of the hurricane." The case of Germán Sánchez—the Cuban ambassador in Venezuela—is one of these. Ever since he came to the country, both his public and private statements would appear destined to stir up a storm. Sánchez is an exceptional mixture of natural Cuban charm and profound political conviction. For that reason, his male and female admirers never fail him, and nor do his detractors, who every once in a while call for his expulsion from Venezuela. That is no easy matter, taking into account the excellent relations between Havana and

Caracas, as well as the total confidence that seems to have been placed in him by Fidel Castro.

Question: How could we define Cuba in the Latin American context?

Germán Sánchez: For me, Cuba is a 100 percent Latin American and Caribbean country. The fact that our people have decided, of their own free will, on an option of social development that in certain aspects is very different from what prevails in the rest of Latin America, does not mean that this presents an obstacle to the collective economic integration process. That epoch has already passed. There may be some outdated prejudices left over from the Cold War, but they are unimportant. Cuba is an open country, with extremely broad relations across the Latin American and Caribbean political spectrum. We share our experience, we study other experiences, and assimilate those that are useful to us. We do not dictate to anyone and neither do we ask anyone to copy us, we simply expect respect and give respect in turn.

The Cuban revolutionary process is unique and unrepeatable; it was born in the vortex of the Cold War, in a polarized world. There is no serious proposal in Venezuela or in any other part of Latin America to copy the Cuban revolution. Each country has its own idea of what should be done, as in the case of Venezuela. Time and time again, President Chávez has affirmed that this is a peaceful and democratic revolutionary process. The Venezuelan constitution has nothing in common with that of a socialist country. Thus, it is not valid to claim that in Venezuela there is a process similar or identical to the Cuban one or that Venezuela is advancing in that direction. The fact that there are aspirations in Chile, Jamaica, Brazil or Venezuela to match our achievements and those of other countries is something else. It is not about wishing to copy a political or economic model, but aspiring to certain results, bearing in mind useful foreign experiences. For example,

Cuba has the dream of being world football champions one day, and in that context, the Brazilian "school" is marvelous. We also aspire to having as much oil as Venezuela, and are working hard to improve the current extraction of our oil by seeking to use the most modern techniques: among others, the innovations made by PDVSA [the Venezuelan state oil company].

Question: What regional integration plans are Cuba involved in, particularly those with CARICOM (The Caribbean Community and Common Market)?

Germán Sánchez: Relations with CARICOM have advanced very well in recent years. The CARICOM member countries have always adopted an attitude of respect, understanding, dialogue and rapprochement with Cuba. In our CARICOM brothers and sisters, we sense the same warm air of the Caribbean. There is a natural disposition to fortify that which unites us and relegate possible differences to a secondary level. This is what links us and makes us a community of countries where an international identity prevails. Caribbean peoples — whether French, English or Spanish speaking — understand each other because we have a very noble and proud concept of our culture and identity.

Question: What is the Cuban position in relation to the United States in the context of what would seem to be a relaxation of the US posture toward the government of Fidel Castro?

Germán Sánchez: We have a realistic position toward the United States. We do not entertain any illusions and are prepared to continue advancing under the current conditions of the blockade. Cuba is experiencing a stage of growth and economic expansion, despite the economic war that the United States continues to wage against us. This war is expressed in many ways, such as the Helms-Burton Act, which prevents any US business from undertaking commercial transactions with Cuba; the aggression of more than 1,500 hours of overtly subversive messages; and the allowing of groups that commit acts of terrorism in Cuba to function on US territory.

In the 1990s the United States mistakenly believed that the "fruit was ripe" and tried to crush us. The failure of that policy has led to a growing current of opinion in the United States promoting different links with us, and the possibility of US citizens being able to travel freely to our territory and to do business. In general, there is a big push in favor of a rapprochement.

The fact that Cuba managed to emerge from its economic crisis and maintain its identity has made us reflect on our options. If moves are made in the right direction, we will sit down and negotiate, but without conditions. If, for example, they file a compensation claim related to the nationalization of US companies which took place from 1959 to 1960, we would have to remind them what really happened. We nationalized the US companies, as we did with Spanish companies and those of other countries. But it was not true, as many people mistakenly believe, that we had no intention of paying for them. We were going to give the owners compensation, although not in the short term. We were a country full of illiterates, we were poor, and we had all kinds of difficulties which needed time to sort out. We talked of paying within 20 years and they did not believe us. They thought that they could destroy us well before that time, and they went down that path. What happened? The Spaniards received money, so did the Canadians and other countries with which we had commitments. It now transpires that, on account of its policy of blockade and aggression, the United States has a debt to Cuba that is far greater than the total value of the businesses nationalized at that time.

Question: And what is the policy in relation to ordinary citizens who lost property in that period?

Germán Sánchez: There were Cuban landowners whose property was taken by the state, in order to give it to the people to work. Now, in the case of those Cubans who have become US citizens, the Helms-Burton Act violates all international jurisprudence by applying retroactivity. Those people who—at that time—were not US citizens, are now pretending to be affected as "US nationals." But let them sit back and wait, because we have drawn up two accounts owing to Cuba: the first totals more than $100 billion due to the effects of the economic blockade; the other, likewise in excess of $100 billion, is based on the damage and material loss caused by US aggression against the Cuban population—for example, in the Bay of Pigs invasion, when hundreds of people were killed or maimed. Thus, just like the United States, we have our own accounts of these 40 years of aggression. They pay us, we pay them and let's see which side the balance favors.

Question: What space does economic freedom occupy on the Cuban agenda?

Germán Sánchez: We think that economic freedom should exist as long as it does not affect the nature of the social system. In our case, economic freedom, free markets—like the agricultural ones—do exist, but the limit begins at the point where the Cuban socialist system is affected, where the concepts of human solidarity are affected, or where equality in the distribution of resources at the social level, such as free education and health care, are affected. In summary, for the Cuban people economic freedom does not mean liberalism but a conscious and deliberate policy that has been put into effect to satisfy the interests of society as a whole and not of a minority.

Letter to Pedro Carmona

Sent by the author to Mr. Pedro Carmona—then president of Fedecámaras (the Venezuelan Federation of Chambers of Industry and Commerce)—on January 23, 2002. In April 2002 Carmona proclaimed himself "president of Venezuela," after a coup d'état organized by the national oligarchy together with certain high-ranking military officers, and with outside backing.

We read with surprise in the Venezuelan press the Fedecámaras communiqué published on Monday, January 21, 2002, which—without any consideration whatsoever—made a fanatical attack on Cuba and its constitutional president, Fidel Castro, with adjectives loaded with hatred and disrespect. We have noted that you have signed such foolish and frenetic accusations "reflections."

We have always had respectful and constructive links with you, avoiding any doctrinaire or political issues, and guided by the sole desire to further mutually beneficial contacts between the entrepreneurs of our two countries. You acted as our host on certain occasions at the Fedecámaras headquarters so that Cuban and Venezuelan entrepreneurs could discuss business opportunities between the two countries. President Fidel Castro himself has met with the Venezuelan business sector—here and in Cuba—in meetings approved and supported by Fedecámaras.

We have not forgotten your presence alongside President Hugo Chávez when you both inaugurated the third exhibition of Cuban products in Venezuela on Tuesday, October 2, 2001, and your words promoting trade and business with Cuba.

When Cuba is recovering economically, how can it be described by Fedecámaras as an isolated, bankrupt nation? It is even harder to understand why you have put your name to that mendacious and McCarthyist text that insinuates that the present Venezuelan government is attempting to imitate the Cuban model, which "would lead the nation into isolation and ruin and stifle freedom..."

Venezuela is not trying to imitate the Cuban model and Cuba is not encouraging it to do so—quite the contrary. Above all, it was Fidel Castro who has emphasized the differences between our processes and systems, just a few hours after Hugo Chávez assumed the presidency on February 3, 1999. On that day, he also found the time to meet with more than 100 Fedecámaras businesspeople and to invite their president at the time, Francisco Natera, to visit Cuba with a large delegation of entrepreneurs. That visit took place, because the Cuban revolution has not closed its doors to the Venezuelan private sector, either under this or prior governments, and will continue promoting relations on respectful and equitable terms.

We asked ourselves: "Why this effort to involve us in the Venezuelan political dispute the day before the anniversary of January 23, 1958 [marking the overthrow of Venezuelan dictator Marcos Pérez Jiménez]? A date that, certainly, was a spur and stimulus to the struggle of our people to achieve their liberty and independence on January 1, 1959, and to foster greater solidarity between the progressive Venezuelan forces and Fidel's Rebel Army in the Sierra Maestra.

It is small-minded—and an insult to the Venezuelan people—to identify the Cuban process with "isolation and ruin." Out of the 189 member countries of the UN, Cuba has diplomatic relations with more than 170—some giants such as China and Brazil have relations with fewer nations—and there are 93 diplomatic missions on Cuban territory. In Cuba there are 155 permanent foreign correspondents from 112 media outlets in 34 countries; more than 400 businesses with foreign capital are operating in Cuba; we receive close to two million foreign visitors every year; moreover, we have commercial links with more than 3,000 foreign companies in 156 countries.

In the last three years, the island has been visited by more than 100 heads of state or government and close to 200 foreign ministers, and has hosted important international forums such as the second South Summit, in which 133 countries took part, and the ninth Ibero-American Summit. Cuba has more than 4,000 professionals and technical personnel collaborating in dozens of Latin American, African and Caribbean nations.

In the last five years, more than 300,000 US citizens have defied the blockade to visit Cuba, at the risk of incurring prison terms and heavy fines. We have also been visited — from the United States — by the president of that country's powerful Chamber of Commerce, dozens of senators and representatives, former high-ranking military officials, hundreds of businesspeople, athletes, academics and students and dozens of artists, actors and prominent intellectuals. Many of them met with Fidel Castro and support doing away with the blockade and the ban on travel to Cuba.

As you can see, Cuba is not isolated, even from US citizens, who evade official restrictions to travel and reduce their stress levels on the streets of the safest country in the world, populated by the most educated, healthy and cultured people of our America.

Blockaded and attacked for more than 40 years, Cuba is recovering strongly and optimistically. For eight consecutive years its economy has been growing, with improvements in efficiency in distinct spheres as well as in human indicators. For example, the infant mortality rate fell to 6.2 per 1,000 live births in 2001, thus overtaking countries like the United States, whose infant mortality rate is 7.0. These days few people would dare to question our advances in health care and education. We do not want to see our model copied, but neither do we wish to be seen as a bad example, and many Cuban experiences — such as the eradication of illiteracy 40 years ago — are recognized at an international level.

Lester Thurow, an eminent professor of economics at the

Massachusetts Institute of Technology, asked in an article how much inequality is acceptable in a democracy. He analyzed the growing disparity in the distribution of wealth within the United States: the accelerated concentration of wealth in the higher levels and the increasing numbers of the dispossessed. Thurow concluded his analysis by comparing US society with the decadence and the collapse of imperial Rome—the most probable fate of the United States if such trends are to continue. We invite you to reflect on this rather than on what Fedecámaras is trying to attribute to Cuba.

The protests in Seattle, Quebec and Genoa were not against communism. As a person who boasts of being a modern thinker, you should dwell on that point, in order to realize that norms different from those of the Cold War and McCarthyism are currently operating. Whoever does not understand this might become an anachronism or truly isolated. In the present-day world, with increasing globalization and diversity, humanism, solidarity and equality have to prevail. There can be no space for egoism or for narrow and sectarian views, as so often displayed in disrespect for the Cuban people.

Cuba—free, independent and sovereign—has chosen a political-social model that is in line with its history, its circumstances and the will of its people, and that is enshrined in a constitution overwhelmingly supported by Cubans in a democratic referendum. The Cuban revolution brought to the island the freedom and dignity that had been lost after half a century of virtual annexation to the United States.

Now we have the authentic and independent system that we wanted for ourselves, and that we have ourselves created. Despite the dogmatic analyses that viewed us as a satellite of Moscow, we survived the collapse of the Soviet Union in 1991, and that of the whole of Eastern Europe. We have successfully passed through, without our supposed mentors and in spite of the empire, another stage in the Cuban revolution. For that reason, we have the moral force to defend our social and political model, and the experience to advise against imitations or copies of it; but, in the same way, nobody should try to force us to adopt a different model. Nobody in the world has the authority to set themselves up as the sole legitimate model, no nation has achieved "total success," and almost all of those who have tried to impose themselves on others have collapsed with time.

We wish Venezuela the greatest success in the construction of a fifth republic that will satisfy the aspirations and dreams of its citizens. We respect the forms that it is adopting to achieve such goals, which have to be the unique creation of its people, without interference and with absolute self-determination. We want the same for Cuba. And for that we ask Fedecámaras for respect.

We hope that your equanimity will allow you to understand our point of view, without the rage that guided the pen of the person who drafted that impertinent communiqué's references to Cuba, which could do so much damage to the institution that you head and the historical links that have existed between our two business communities.

Non-diplomatic responses
(Interview with *El Nacional*, April 24, 2003)

Question: The recent imprisonment of members of the Cuban opposition even provoked the condemnation of figures such as the writer José Saramago and sectors that traditionally support Cuba. Why was this measure taken?

Germán Sánchez: The question includes certain value judgments that are necessary to clarify. These decisions, adopted by our courts in a sovereign manner, in which impunity does not reign, have been criticized—above all—by the large international disinformation mechanisms controlled by the United States. And similarly in other countries where the current of opinion designed and promoted from those centers of global power has been reflected. Any sensible journalist knows that this is the case. Some responses have been publicized, such as that of Saramago. His statement has gone around the world.

Question: And that of Eduardo Galeano?

Germán Sánchez: And Galeano's. They are the most prominent two. However, I have not read here in Venezuela, nor have I seen reflected on CNN the opinions of Mario Benedetti or Heinz Dieterich, to mention two examples, or those of dozens of other intellectuals and political and social leaders around the world.

I ask myself: Why the discrimination against so many figures who are defending those sovereign Cuban decisions? Once again the intentions of those who hold power in the United States have been demonstrated. The advances that they have already made through the transnational corporations, their powerful military resources and their great apparatuses for shaping public opinion are not enough for them, and now, they have decided to destroy any kind of obstacle that is placed in the way of their pretension to complete global domination.

If we look at what is occurring in Iraq, I think there is general agreement throughout the world that it is a war of pillage, seeking, in the first place, to appropriate that country's oil and the control of energy in the Middle East—at any cost in terms of human lives and the destruction of infrastructure and buildings that are of tremendous cultural value to humanity. Of course, the war also affects the Organization of the Petroleum Exporting Countries (OPEC), which is not playing along with US geopolitical domination in that region or elsewhere on the planet.

Question: Of course, but...

Germán Sánchez: Excuse me, I will "land" on your question shortly. First, it is important "to fly a little bit higher," in order to see what is happening from above and to comprehend that we are not in just any moment in the history of humanity.

We are living at a time when the superpower has unleashed all its force and brutality in an attempt to secure total domination of the planet, even at the price of destroying Iraq and fragmenting the already extremely weak and steadily worsening United Nations.

That great power is also attempting to seize control of Cuba, because that has always been its intention, since before 1959. Now it is utilizing more direct methods, as stated clearly in the Helms-Burton Act of 1996, which legalizes in the United States the project of imposing an economic and political regime on Cuba that responds totally to US interests and dictates.

That great power has begun to practice a neofascist foreign policy, undeterred by the United Nations or its European allies, other continents, or global public opinion. This same superpower, now directed by people with an interventionist and fascist mentality, has designed a plan of aggression against Cuba, to "pounce" at the moment it considers appropriate.

We Cubans, who know US imperialism very well, who know exactly which way they will jump, and how they might trip up or have difficulties advancing their interests, prioritize exposing the background to US actions. The failure of US policy has a lot to do with the global resistance that is opposed to it, given that no country is exempt from the danger it poses for humanity.

Geographically, Cuba is close to the United States and has suffered a blockade, an economic siege, for more than 40 years. We have been the victim of various acts of terrorism that have cut short the lives of more than 3,500 Cubans: an invasion in 1961 and acts of biological warfare that, on more than one occasion, have transmitted diseases to our edible plants and animals in order to affect the country's economy and Cuban lives. We have been systematically subjected to more than 1,200 hours per week of radio broadcasts, and a television transmission, financed to the tune of $30 million per annum, whose signal cannot be picked up in Cuba due to our technicians blocking it. There is a constant project to poison and distort reality with the aim of wearing down the Cuban revolutionary process. This is from the same power that has utilized the blockade and emigration as weapons of its policy to isolate and subvert Cuba.

The Bush government has decided — as part of its global aggressive and neofascist policy — to destroy the Cuban revolutionary process and the social system freely chosen by our people many years ago. One principal instrument being utilized to that end is the US Interests Section in Havana. This Interests Section was created — by mutual agreement between Jimmy Carter and our government — in 1976, and has limited and well-defined functions. As in the case of any diplomatic representation, in line with the Vienna Convention that determines relations between states, it cannot in any way involve itself in the internal affairs of the country in which it is accredited, and certainly not conspire with certain citizens to overthrow the government and political system decided on by the sovereign will of the people.

Why were these 75 Cuban citizens arrested, tried and sentenced? They were arrested and tried by our courts in accordance with the legal regulations of our country, and sentenced to various prison terms — one by one — not because their opinions are different from the political regime or the prevailing politics in Cuba. Nobody in Cuba is tried or sent to prison for dissenting, for thinking differently. Dissent is an intrinsic right of Cuban citizens according to the constitution and the law. In Cuba, if one thing exists, it is respect for individual thinking.

What this is about is that these 75 people were caught in flagrante, acting in a conspiratorial manner. In the first place, with Mr. James Cason, head of the Interests Section, and later with other

US diplomatic officials. And when I say "acting in a conspiratorial manner," I am referring to the fact that these individuals, as proven by the courts, decided to join this Interests Section and its head to defeat the government of Cuba—not by acting through the political system that allows them to stand as candidates in the elections and to advance their positions and their ideas, if they were accepted by the population. No, they simply acted with the aim of creating the conditions for applying the Helms-Burton Act. And when we talk of the Helms-Burton Act, I reiterate that it is not just an interventionist law that blockades our country's economy, but it is also one through which the United States has attributed to itself the right to intervene in Cuba's internal affairs, to utilize millions and millions of dollars every year for subversion and to act against Cuba in an overt and undisguised way.

With overwhelming evidence—signed documents, tape recordings and the statements of witnesses—it was confirmed that these "gentlemen" were acting in the service of US policy and conspiring with Mr. James Cason as part of the plan to overthrow the Cuban revolution and the state constituted by our people. How did they do that? They met with Cason and other officials, and they received instructions, political and conspiratorial material and money to execute those plans. Their financial support totaled a few million dollars.

Those trials complied with legal regulations, as is always the case in Cuba, where there is no impunity and no corrupt judges or district attorneys, and where the law is applied in an appropriate and rigorous manner. It has been demonstrated that those 75 individuals are not the dissidents that they have been portrayed as.

Question: What are they then?

Germán Sánchez: They are mercenaries, because they received money and acted in a conspiratorial manner with the representatives of a foreign power to defeat a legitimate national government.

In such a way that, for example, if this had occurred in the United States, if it was the reverse, if a group of citizens in coordination with a diplomatic representation in the United States—that of Cuba, Venezuela, Russia or France—and with its ambassador, if that ambassador had called on a group of 75 US citizens and told them: "We're going to defeat the Bush government, here's so much money, we have to act in this manner, we have to unite among ourselves to achieve that proposition," the United States—as it has done on other occasions, utilizing its national security laws— would have imposed even more severe sanctions. An example is what happened with the Rosenbergs, unjustly sentenced to death for allegedly being the agents of a foreign power.

No country with self-respect, no government with authority, and no place where laws exist could allow a conspiratorial move-ment to be organized and financed from a foreign embassy to defeat a legitimately constituted government. That is a basic prin-ciple of international law and the laws of any country. What Cuba did was to apply the law…

Question: Should the Venezuelan government follow Cuba's example and begin to detain opponents?

Germán Sánchez: The Venezuelan government and the Bolivarian revolutionary process in Venezuela is indigenous and original, its grandeur is rooted there and it is for the people to decide what happens in Venezuela.

I would like to discuss the question of the "Cubanization" of Venezuela. The resort to this argument is an expression of weakness, not strength, by the proponents of this campaign. Why? They apparently fear Venezuela's historical potential and the uniqueness of the Bolivarian revolution. Venezuelans made that revolution; it has emerged from Venezuela's history.

It is absurd to persist in comparing Venezuela and its revol-utionary process with Cuba. I will give you three facts. The Cuban revolutionary process began in 1953. Fidel Castro was 26 at that time. Young people like you attacked a military garrison on July 26, 1953, and initiated a revolution against the criminal dictatorship of Fulgencio Batista, who had usurped power just a year before. Civilians went to assault the garrison—not to kill soldiers—but with the aim of seizing weapons and giving them to the people. Here in Venezuela—as far as I know—it was the reverse. It was young soldiers who decided to attack the civil power, which— according to them—was a corrupt and antidemocratic power. In other words, the Cuban revolutionary process had a different birth to that in Venezuela.

Furthermore, in 1959, how did the Cuban revolution come to power? By popular violence: with weapons in hand the people managed to defeat the army and the dictatorship. No prisoner was shot; wounded prisoners were treated and released—the reverse of what happened to our prisoners. The dictatorship tortured and killed more than 20,000 Cubans. That is why we have so much respect for the life, honor and dignity of human beings. And it is for that reason that in revolutionary Cuba nobody has ever been kidnapped or disappeared, as has been the case under so many dictatorships and in many other countries; and neither have any members of the police force taken the law into their own hands and killed a criminal outside of the law. In Cuba, the law and the judges function properly and are not corrupted. We respect one another—that is how we won the revolution.

In Venezuela, how did the Bolivarian process achieve government? Through arms? No, with votes! Thus, the way the two processes came to power is also quite different.

Now, if we compare the two constitutions, there are also important differences. Twenty-six months after the triumph of the revolution in Cuba, the ownership of property had been radically transformed. Education was free to everybody, as was health care. The literacy campaign was completed by the end of 1961. Rents were initially reduced by 50 percent and then the people gained ownership of their homes. Cubans' lives were transformed in a myriad of ways.

Currently, Venezuela is experiencing a process of change at a different pace and in different circumstances. Within 26 months the opposition in Cuba had left to become an appendage of the United States, where they continued to conspire. There were invasions and acts of terrorism and subversion against the revolutionary process. There is no comparison between what is happening today in Venezuela and what happened in Cuba in the early years of the revolution. So why insist on this?

Question: No, excuse me, but "Cubanization" relates to two points... First, the fact that President Chávez says he wants to remain in power until 2021 — retention of power similar to that of President Castro. And second, even if the economic system enshrined in the Venezuelan constitution allows for private property, it is no less a fact that the state presence is excessive and there is a desire to consolidate the concept of the state as the owner of the economy.

Germán Sánchez: I respect your opinion, but really it is not accurate. In Cuba, the people own the means of production. And moreover, there are a larger number of proprietors in Cuba than in Venezuela or in any other country on the continent. Did you know that?

Question: There are more private property owners?

Germán Sánchez: Yes. The Cuban revolution generated more property owners than before the triumph of the revolution, and many more than currently exist in Venezuela. I will explain:

In terms of Cuban homes, 85 percent of them are owned by the families living in them. And land? Eighty percent is state owned, but a good part of it has been handed over in indefinite usufruct to cooperatives, which own the produce. There are also 100,000 small individual proprietors of land, not to mention the factories that are the property of the people, and the schools and hospitals that belong to the people...

Question: Good, but that is what President Chávez is saying. President Chávez wants the workers to be the owners of enterprises. He wants to develop a very strong economy based on cooperatives.

Germán Sánchez: Are you familiar with state capitalism? Did you know that in Argentina, before the advent of neoliberalism, and in Chile, before neoliberalism dismantled the state capitalist properties, and in Mexico, there were a vast number of state properties? Railroads, buses, energy installations and airlines — far more than in Venezuela. Did it ever occur to anyone, before the Cuban revolution was born, to say that Perón was going to make a socialist revolution [in Argentina]? One has to know history.

Now, if you are defending capitalism, out-and-out private property, individual profit above any other value — "Long live the rich and never mind the poor!" — then we should end this discussion. But, if you are defending a concept of equity, of humanism in its real sense, you cannot say that the state, in a capitalist or socialist regime, has no role as an instrument of the sovereign will of the nation.

And there can be variants within capitalism, because neoliberalism is not the same as capitalism, which has different options and models. Neoliberalism is not the same as state capitalism. The capitalism of Keynes is not that of Milton Friedman and the Chicago School. Thus, history cannot be reduced to what is happening today. It has to be seen in its evolution and diversity. Sweden is not the same as Chile, where state ownership is being dismantled.

Please don't confuse state social action with socialism. Capitalism invented the social function of the state before socialism existed.

Question: Now, if we are not moving toward a Cuban model, what are so many Cuban officials doing here? Everyone is talking about them, but the total number is never revealed. Can you tell us about that? How many are there? What are they doing, where are they? Who are they? Who is paying them?

Germán Sánchez: I wrote an article called "Permission to express an opinion on Cuba" that was published in *El Nacional* in 2000, in the midst of a furious campaign against my country that continues today. There was the story of 1,500 Cuban agents infiltrated into all the garrisons, headed by Álvaro Rosabal, the Cuban "James Bond." A huge scandal. It emerged that Rosabal was a fraud, and a week later, he said that he had been conned by two Miami terrorist mercenaries, Venezuelan lawyer Ricardo Koesling and ex-Batista police agent Salvador Romaní, who had promised him—in Caracas—money to go to the United States. The story collapsed and nobody said anything more about the matter!

Then they proceeded to say that the Venezuelan constitution was the same as Cuba's. Fidel Castro even invited a group of Venezuelan journalists to the island to explain the differences between the two constitutions. They wanted to say that the constitution on which people would vote in the 1999 referendum was the same as that of Cuba, and moreover, that Chávez was attempting to lead Venezuela toward communism. Actually, these little campaigns have been somewhat exhausted. I think they will have to look for other issues, because it is absurd to continue lying to the Venezuelan people, every day, about the same thing.

Then in December 2002, during the coup-organized oil strike, Carlos Ortega appeared every day on the private television networks, declaring: "The *Pilín León* [boat] has been moved by agents of Castro-communism, by Cuban marines." The lie was exposed within a few hours, when the marines declared that they were Venezuelan. The next day, I was waiting for the long nose of Carlos Ortega to bump into the TV cameras. No, he avoided the issue, nothing happened. So, yet another media lie got no kind of retraction.

Question: So, there are no Cuban officials in Venezuela?

Germán Sánchez: First, I would like to say—before answering you—that this campaign of calumnies and falsehoods is really abominable. Fortunately, the Venezuelan people know its instigators and can see what they are made of, the people know their backgrounds and have been able to see, time and time again, that these lies collapse against the facts and what is really happening. Further, it seems to me that the time has come to suggest to the creators of this campaign that they try to find another story, because the one about "Cubanization" is not working.

The Venezuelan people feel closer and closer to Cuba. See how strange that is. This has turned into a boomerang: Every day Venezuelans stop us in the street, express their solidarity more directly, mobilize when necessary, and sympathize more with Cuba because now they know the truth. If they are told: "The Cuban doctors are agents," the people don't believe it, because they are experiencing the services of our physicians and can confirm their professional and humanitarian qualities.

Question: Are there 300 of them?

Germán Sánchez: The exact figure is announced on a daily basis, because—among other reasons—journalists, without realizing it, are often victims of the campaigns orchestrated by the media. I believe that journalism is about investigating, reasoning, seeking out the truth and not being duped by manipulators who are always inventing one tall tale or another.

That data is offered every day in our embassy and publicized through our bulletins and a webpage; and we give interviews. We have nothing to hide, because we feel very satisfied and proud of the support and the solidarity that we have been giving to Venezuelans for many years, not just now in the Chávez period. That is something else that we should clarify: relations between Venezuela and Cuba did not begin recently, but in the 19th century, with mutual support. That sisterhood has a long history, nobody can eclipse it, because it is too beautiful, too solid and too sublime to be falsified in any manner.

Question: There has been talk of certain episodes…

Germán Sánchez: Afterwards we can discuss any episode that you want. Do you want to know how the cooperation between Venezuela and Cuba is going? Excellently, it is advancing very well, better every day.

Question: But what is it that they are doing?

Germán Sánchez: Shall I explain it in detail? Let's start with health. Since the cooperation agreement between Cuba and Venezuela was signed, thousands of poor sick people — those who die at the entrances of hospitals because they lack the money for an operation or for complex treatment — have gone to Cuba. There they have received attention in Cuban hospitals completely free of charge, from the finest specialists, and a large percentage of them have returned cured or in much better health. This has been shown, in part, on television, and here is the list, if you want, so that you can go to see and interview the people yourself. We feel very proud of being able to help the poor people of Venezuela who do not otherwise have access to these resources.

At this moment, we have hundreds of doctors here in nine

states of the country. They are not solely in the states where there is a government that sympathizes with the Bolivarian process, there are Cuban doctors where there are mayors with other political affiliations. It does not matter. It was our decision and that of the Chávez government not to discriminate against anybody, because we came here to help Venezuelan citizens without regarding their religious beliefs, the color of their skin or their political position. They are human beings in need of support. Where are those doctors? Replacing Venezuelan doctors? No, they are complementing the work of the doctors here, they are working where there are no Venezuelan doctors, and that is a condition of our lending services in Venezuela or in any other country of the world.

Some people said: "They are going to Cubanize us because so many of them have come." Well, are they also "Cubanizing" Guatemala, Haiti, Gambia? What is this "Cubanization?" It is about helping people in need. We have the highest proportion of doctors in the world: one for every 166 Cubans. We have trained tens of thousands of young people who have, moreover, an ethical education: they seek to serve their neighbors and not to use them for their own ends, and that has a value that is even greater than scientific training, which they also have. Well, that is "Cubanization." Ask the Venezuelan people if they want that "Cubanization."

Question: Are we on to education?

Germán Sánchez: No, we are still discussing health. In the last three years we have been exporting to Venezuela — at prices below those of the world market — more than $40 million worth of generic medicines, which complement those manufactured here. These were previously imported by Venezuela from other countries and now they are imported from Cuba, with the same quality and at lower cost.

Question: And who is paying for that?

Germán Sánchez: These are paid for by the government of Venezuela—only the medicines, not the doctors, who are totally free of charge.

Question: And who pays the travel costs?

Germán Sánchez: The cost of transporting patients is paid by Venezuela. In the case of transporting doctors, sometimes Cuba, sometimes Venezuela, that depends.

We have also exported high-quality medical equipment: electro-cardiograms, laboratories, etc.

Cuba is a world-renowned medical power, and so why wouldn't Venezuela utilize those strengths of a sister people, geographically close, with the same language, and who have a readiness to cooperate without profiteering?

Who can criticize that? Isn't it absurd to oppose Cuba offering and exporting—at half or a third of the market price—anti-AIDS treatments?

Question: And in education?

Germán Sánchez: In education there has been some consulting in certain specialties, like special education and literacy. We have offered hundreds of scholarships and have received in Cuba more than 450 students of medicine in the last four years. More than 250 students are studying for a degree in sports and physical education.

Question: Is that being paid for by the Venezuelan government?

Germán Sánchez: That is being totally covered by the Cuban government: accommodation and food, clothing, textbooks, medical attention and recreation. The Venezuelan government only pays for the transportation. There are a few thousand Latin

Americans on similar scholarships studying medicine, and another few thousand in sports and physical education and other professions. We are poor, but grateful. Cuba can never repay its debt of gratitude with the poor of the earth, who have always given us their solidarity.

Question: And in terms of security?

Germán Sánchez: I will respond to that later. To continue, there are postgraduate students who are being paid for by the Venezuelan government under the cooperation agreement. There are a few dozen students studying for doctorates in various disciplines, according to needs defined by the Venezuelan state.

Question: In relation to sports, in an interview that I did with Minister Marta Lomas, she said that Cuba had paid—up to the end of 2001—$200 million in relation to the oil agreement, but that Venezuela owed Cuba for the trainers. I would like to know if Venezuela has already paid Cuba.

Germán Sánchez: Yes, of course. I will fully explain the sports issue. At this moment we have 740 high-performance sports instructors and others working as physical education and recreation teachers. All of them have degrees, they are in 21 Venezuelan states, in more than 170 municipalities, fulfilling social functions under the plans of the councils and government of Venezuela. If you want an opinion on these teachers, I invite you to visit Apure, Barinas, there in Lara, here in Vargas and throughout Caracas, and ask people. Do you know how many pupils they have? They have 600,000, who in one way or another are receiving the universal benefits of sport. That is the "Cubanization" they are receiving, the help of Olympic champions. There are Olympic champion boxers here, and baseball players who recently lost against a team on which Chávez played, because they are elderly now. In other words, we are giving Venezuela the best of Cuban medicine, the best of Cuban sports. I don't suppose people will be upset by this "Cubanization."

Question: How much has the Venezuelan government paid the Cuban government for that collaboration?

Germán Sánchez: Not much, I can tell you. The total for the technical services was around $5.5 million for 600 sports instructors for one year. If they were US sports instructors, not even $100 million would cover their costs.

Question: Will that collaboration continue?

Germán Sánchez: We are going to carry on, because the collaboration is significant and important, and it will grow. This is to Venezuela's benefit: those sports instructors, like the doctors, are benefiting the Venezuelan people.

Question: In agriculture, what is the sum and in which area is it centered?

Germán Sánchez: In agriculture the Barinas agribusiness complex is a top priority. That institution is going to be the most modern in South America and will generate more than 9,000 direct and indirect jobs in agriculture and industry...

Question: And who is putting up the money for that? Venezuela or Cuba?

Germán Sánchez: Cuba is supporting the project and the technical planning. Of course, Venezuela will benefit from the project, as well as Brazil. The technology for this industrial complex is going to be purchased there, given that Brazil is a leader in sugarcane technology. The country that is going to benefit—in terms of economic profit—from the complex is Venezuela. Then comes Brazil. Cuba is to modestly contribute the know-how of its technical personnel, who come from a 200-year tradition of sugar cultivation on the island.

Other consultancies in agriculture are anticipated. For example, a program of urban farms and intensive gardens is already underway under the framework of the UN Food and Agriculture Organization (FAO), funded by Venezuela and the FAO. Cuba is contributing specialists, without charging any fees. High-level Cuban technicians and scientists are backing that program in Caracas and Margarita and it will be extended later to other cities. Cuba, the country to have most developed those techniques in recent years, is offering its experiences and all the support needed to Venezuela in solidarity, without any gain. Do you know how many jobs those cultivation plots have generated in Cuba in barely eight years? More than 326,000, almost the same number as those within traditional agriculture. That is why the FAO, through its secretary general, asked us to offer assistance to Venezuela.

Question: When the people talk of "Cubanization," I think that the most worrying aspect is not related to economics, agriculture, health or sports, but is related to security agents, to intelligence. Do you deny that there are Cuban security agents operating in Venezuela at this moment?

Germán Sánchez: What does "security agents" mean? I don't understand, please define the term.

Question: Cuban state security agents.

Germán Sánchez: From Cuba? But how are we going to have state security agents here?

Question: Do you deny it?

Germán Sánchez: How are we going to have state security agents in a sister country? Nations have security agents where there is a force or a country that has an aggressive attitude. So, why would we have security agents in Venezuela?

Question: But, are you denying it?

Germán Sánchez: Of course. What we have here are agents of health, agents of sports, agents of education, sugarcane agents, agents who, simply, are contributing to the development, well-being and happiness of the Venezuelan people.

Question: For example, it has been said that President Chávez's entire security team is composed of Cuban agents.

Germán Sánchez: Do you know why that is being said? It would seem to be on account of the racism prevailing among a small group of Venezuelans, because for the first time—I don't know about in the past—not just one but several black people have been included in that security team, and apparently there are no black Venezuelans. So those defamers and obsessed individuals— some of them psychiatric cases—assume those black people, or all black people in the world today, are Cubans. Therefore, Mr. Churio, the chief of Chávez's bodyguards, who is black, "must be a Cuban." Due to their pathological, almost comical obsession, those gentlemen imagine they are Cubans because they are black. They forget that there are many black people in Venezuela as well. Their prejudice has resulted in a ridiculous defamation campaign.

Question: Are you meddling in the Venezuelan situation? Are you violating the Vienna Convention, which determines up to what point a diplomat should or should not express opinions or act in another country?

Germán Sánchez: Have you read the Vienna Convention? I am going to give you a copy, I want you to quote from it in this interview, because it states expressly that diplomats accredited in the receiving country, in this case Cuban diplomats accredited in Venezuela, have the right to defend their country's interests. Also, to defend their citizens living in that country, correct? Without violating the laws of that country, of course. If anyone began to attack Venezuela in Cuba or in the United States and started to slander its government or to fabricate lies hundreds of thousands of times as part of a systematic campaign, the Venezuelan ambassador has the right, under the Vienna Convention—as I did in 2000 and as I do every time it is necessary—to defend his or her country in the face of those calumnies. That is not interference in internal affairs, that is defending your country's interests and your compatriots. It is protected by international law, specifically in the Vienna Convention.

I have responded to the opposition deputy, Gerardo Blyde, and certain others. The people of Venezuela are the ones to have the last word, and the reality is different to what is said in those campaigns. Mr. Gerardo Blyde complained: "The Cuban ambassador interfered in internal affairs." What right does Mr. Gerardo Blyde have to say that Cuban sports instructors or Cuban doctors are living like slaves? What right does he have to bad mouth human beings who are living here in solidarity to serve the Venezuelan people? None. But I do have the right to defend our citizens, and for that reason, I responded to him. He got annoyed because I told the truth, and he invoked international law, and I responded again and said to him: "Look, read the Vienna Convention, you believe you are a good lawyer, so you should recall that the Vienna Convention gives me the right to defend Cuban citizens in Venezuela and to defend my homeland, my country that is constantly being vilified by a group of individuals who have access to the media. And I will continue doing so."

The truth about Cuba will be circulated and not only by me. It has been proclaimed by many Venezuelans who also have access to the press, by Cuban diplomats, and by others, like those who recently came here for the world solidarity with Cuba conference. Certain individuals made a big fuss in the press because on that occasion, Cuban children and young people sang and demonstrated what Cuba is really like, and those individuals do not like their lies exposed. We have the right to talk about Cuba in Venezuela, in China, and even in the United States. Nobody can stop us, it is legal, it is legitimate. We will continue doing so. Now, there are other ambassadors here and you should ask them, because I read them in the press regularly and see them on television recommending what should be done.

Question: Like who?

Germán Sánchez: The ambassador of the United States.

Question: Do you believe that he has violated the Vienna Convention?

Germán Sánchez: I believe that any diplomat, whether the ambassador of the United States or another country, who expresses opinions about what should be done within the reality of a country — be it Venezuela or Cuba — as they have been doing, is in violation of the Vienna Convention. The case of Cuba is far more serious, because they have been conspiring. Any ambassador can offer an opinion on their own country, they have the right to do so, to defend the interests of their homeland; but no ambassador has the right to tell one party or another what it should be doing and how it should resolve its conflicts.

Question: Do you think that Ambassador Shapiro is acting here as Mr. James Cason is doing in Havana?

Germán Sánchez: No, I don't believe that. That is what *you* are saying.

Question: Well, I am asking you.

Germán Sánchez: What I am saying is that when an opinion is expressed on Venezuelan domestic matters, the Vienna Convention is being violated, whoever the ambassador.

Question: Regarding the April activities, the Cuban government brought a girl of 12, who accused the opposition and the media of organizing the coup. Isn't that interference?

Germán Sánchez: I don't recall the terms in which she said that. But it is a fact that children in Cuba are citizens who think, who have the right to express opinions, and who are free to make their own judgments. Children in Cuba are taught to think for themselves. They are shown what is happening in the world, because you cannot say: "From this point, when you are 18, I am going to teach you that the United States is the enemy of Cuba, that it wishes to destroy the schools in which you are studying without charge and convert them into private schools, and that when you go to hospital, if you have money they will let you in, but if you don't you could die." Those children are developing intellectually and emotionally. They are taught the truth about our history, our country and the world through the media and their education, making them thinking beings.

Why should you be surprised that boys or girls of 12 can have their own point of view?

They were not brought by the Cuban embassy, it was a delegation of youth, children, athletes and scientists. Olympic champions have been here too as representatives of our people. What did they come for? Because we were happy at the first anniversary of the Venezuelan people's victory over fascism. How could we not be happy, when we were the victims of fascism: they nearly made a violent assault on this embassy, like a pack of human hounds.

We were happy because, on that April 12, 2002, that girl, who was 11 at the time, probably saw on television what was happening here and could see who those fascists were. That girl—Patricia— was here for the decoration of all the embassy compañeros who defended Cuba's honor on behalf of our people when fascists attacked us. She came and spoke on behalf of the children of Cuba, she spoke from her heart. She expressed herself without any notes in her hands... In December and January, that girl saw what happened in Venezuela during the strike, because the Cuban people were informed of all this. I do not wish to interfere in Venezuela's affairs, you are the ones who have to describe them, but what was happening in Venezuela was shown and explained to the people of Cuba. Everything that happened: the permanent private TV channels with no commercials, Ortega saying that President Chávez would fall the next day... So, that 12-year-old girl, who is a thinking being and should not be underestimated, drew her own conclusion and expressed her opinion. It is said that there are two kinds of people who speak the truth: drunks, because they are uninhibited, and children. Thus, José Martí taught us that children are the hope of the world, children are those who know how to love, and they are very often those who speak the truth, because they do not make compromises.

Question: So she spoke the truth?

Germán Sánchez: And she was not brought here by the Cuban embassy. She came because, simply, the Cuban people are in solidarity with the people of Venezuela and sent their representatives to share the victory of the Bolivarian people of Venezuela on April 13, 2002. This did not please certain people. We are very sorry about that. But it is a fact that various people are lying every day about Cuba. One group—I am not saying the entire opposition.

We have relations here with a large section of the opposition. We are talking now about a pro-coup sector, which is the same group consistently acting against Cuba as well. The terrorists that came here to attack this embassy, who cut off our electricity and water, who represented the supposed humanist, democratic sector, committed all those crimes. We are talking about the people who supported them and we know very well who the super-democrats, super-humanists are, given that they revealed themselves as fascists and terrorists. That sector is not worthy of our praise; rather, we simply told our people who they are, and that girl watched the footage of her compatriots being attacked by a group of pro-coup fascists.

Question: But she was talking about the media. Does the Cuban government consider the Venezuelan media to be pro-coup?

Germán Sánchez: I am not describing the Venezuelan media as pro-coup; what I am saying is that it is for you to reach a conclusion on certain things that happened in Venezuela in the month of April 2002, and which continued in December of that year and in January 2003.

Another thing: in April 2002, besieged in our embassy, we were at the point of being assaulted by those human bloodhounds, at the point where everyone inside, including children and women, could have been killed. In those dramatic circumstances, the press didn't want to publicize our situation. There was one television channel — Globovisión — that interviewed me and Baltazar Porras, the president of the Episcopal Conference, whom we let in. We talked to Globovisión about the possibility of an exclusive, two interviews, but they decided not to broadcast them, and when I asked for a copy for our files, on Monday, April 15, they replied that they had copied something else on top of them. So, I have experienced here the complicity of a lot of the media with the April coup organizers. I am stating that because we experienced it, and it has been confirmed by the press agencies and foreign correspondents here. The media blackout of what occurred in Venezuela on April 12 and 13 has been affirmed throughout the world. It is up to you to describe them as coup plotters or not. I am describing a fact. We were victims of brutal censorship—which only occurs in fascist countries—during April 12 and 13, 2002.

I am friends with certain editors, I have very good friends among journalists and I respect the profession of journalism. I have good relations with many Venezuelan journalists, who have done excellent interviews with me—like the one you are doing today—who are fulfilling their duty. That is one thing, but its another thing entirely to not recognize what the entire planet has said and knows: that from April 12 to April 13, 2002, a large part of the Venezuelan media concealed the truth from the people of Venezuela and the world. At the end of the day, it is you who have to make a judgment on that.

Question: Ambassador, you have just stated that you have very good relations with a sector of the opposition. Which sector is that?

Germán Sánchez: With the sector that respects us, which is a large part.

Question: But which part?

Germán Sánchez: Well, we have relations with AD, Unión, COPEI and Proyecto Venezuela, for example. We have links today that date back many years. We share our mutual truths, we talk and they know how we think.

Question: And with Primero Justicia [Justice First]?

Germán Sánchez: It is impossible to only have relations with sectors that do not criticize you, because the world of today is full of criticisms and counter-criticisms. That is pluralism and we accept that. That isn't the issue. What we reject is the posture of a sector that not only criticizes, but deliberately and consciously lies and acts to create the conditions for aggression against Cuba, and to provoke actions like those perpetrated against our embassy in April. A woman like Ruth Capriles cannot be our friend, neither can I have cordial relations with her, a woman who says that she is the president of an organization of prophets, and who stood before a meeting in Chuao on Tuesday, April 9, 2002 — the same location from where the coup march of April 11 set off — fully broadcast on television, and claimed that men with black bags loaded with weapons were leaving the Cuban embassy. She provoked immediate violence, with Molotov cocktails and shots being fired outside the embassy at 2:00 a.m., thus creating the conditions for the subsequent attacks on April 12. Is she a member of the opposition? I don't know. I am talking of the legitimate opposition, the sensible opposition, the civilized opposition, the opposition that states its point of view, that acts in politics as one should act, within the framework of the law, the constitution, respect for others' rights — which is peace, as Benito Juárez said. We have relations with that opposition, we communicate, we talk, we understand each other, despite our differences. Lamentably, during the escalating conflict — from 1999 to 2003 — a large part of that opposition was eclipsed by the most reactionary sectors, which on many occasions dragged it into coup-type adventures.

I have friends in the opposition. And when they invite me to a political event, to attend like any other ambassador in the world, I go. Salas Römer invited me to the Eurobuilding Hotel, to a political activity involving hundreds of people from the opposition. Some of them were surprised to see me. Why not? I have known Salas Römer for more than eight years, from when he was governor of Carabobo. Why would I not listen to him? Why isolate myself? I have the right to be informed, which is a principle of the Vienna Convention. Ambassadors and diplomats have the right to be informed of what is going on in the country where they are accredited. It was for that reason that I went to the Proyecto Venezuela party's activity. Afterwards, the Patria para

Todos [Homeland for All] party, who support Chávez, invited me and I went to their event as well. Why not? If I go to the Proyecto Venezuela event and the Patria para Todos event, why should I not go to any activity to which I am invited? Primero Justicia invited me in April 2002, after the coup.

Julio Borges, president of Primero Justicia, cordially invited me by letter—in April 2002—to the headquarters of that party! Good grief! The mayor, Capriles Radonski—the leader of Primero Justicia—acted on April 12 in a manner that I do not wish to describe because you already know what happened. He did not protect this embassy. On his orders, the police stood back and allowed what took place to happen. Afterwards, he came into the embassy and belligerently pressured me to allow a search of our headquarters, in blatant violation of the Vienna Convention. I have a recording of that dialogue with me, thanks to a television channel. Despite that, a few days later, Julio Borges invited me to the meeting along with other ambassadors. Why wouldn't I go there? They invited me cordially, and I went there and I listened.

That is our position. Let nobody say that we are against the opposition. We respect Venezuela's internal political life and have links with the Venezuelan opposition. Naturally, we maintain a close and fraternal relationship with this government, because it has facilitated a deepening of the historical relations between Venezuela and Cuba. During the second mandate of Carlos Andrés Pérez, from 1990 to 1992, and afterwards with Caldera, a total of 19 agreements and accords on cooperation, trade, promotion and protection of investments were signed here. There were exchanges. Our foreign minister came here, yours went to Cuba, agreements were signed, trade relations grew. When Chávez won in 1998, Venezuela was already Cuba's biggest trading partner, largely because of our purchases of oil.

Chávez didn't discover Cuba, nor did Cuba discover Venezuela with Chávez. There is a long history of relations. So, let's not have any more distortions of reality. We are not enemies of the opposition. Quite the opposite: we respect those who respect us. But we repudiate fascists and we will fight them on any terrain: that of ideas, and if they give us trouble in another area, we shall respond in kind. We challenge fascism and terrorism, we criticize it, we confront it and we will always confront it. Fascism arose here, this was clearly evident on April 11 and 12 in Venezuela. What we experienced in our embassy is one thing, and the democratic, respectful and civilized opposition of Venezuela is another. We have highly diverse, and in some cases frequent links with that opposition.

Question: President Hugo Chávez often mentions his conversations with President Fidel Castro. Do you think that the antipathy toward Cuba, which I do not want to characterize or quantify, is in part the result of those talks? How often do they talk?

Germán Sánchez: First, it is normal that two heads of state should talk. For example, I believe that President Chávez has met more times with the president of Colombia during this period than with President Fidel Castro. Moreover, from what I have heard from President Chávez, he has personal relations with many other OPEC and Latin American presidents. For example, previously with Cardoso, and now with Lula [President Luiz Inácio Lula da Silva of Brazil]. He did an "Aló presidente" ["Hello President" — Chávez's regular television program] in Guatemala. As I understand, President Chávez is noted for his very active, diverse and broad foreign policy, so why do they pay so much attention to his relations with Fidel? It stems from the prejudices of one sector of the opposition, and the plan is to utilize those relations to defame Cuba and President Chávez. Why should the links between two heads of state, who knew each other before one of them became president — since 1994 — provoke such criticism?

That friendship favors both peoples and is part of the close sisterhood that has existed between Venezuela and Cuba since the 19th century. The problem is that the United States wants Cuba to be isolated, and it must have hit them hard that President Chávez has included our country in the Caracas Energy Agreement. Cuba is in the Caribbean, not in the Caspian Sea, and Venezuela has a policy toward the Caribbean and Central America, so it is logical that we too should be the beneficiaries of a Venezuelan policy toward all the countries in the region. In turn, Cuba has much to contribute to Venezuela in the social and scientific-technical fields.

The Helms-Burton Act attempts to prevent any kind of egalitarian treatment of Cuba. But Venezuela is a sovereign country, and Chávez is its president. He has exercised the sovereignty that this people gave him when they made him president. Does that hurt the United States and its allies in Venezuela? Too bad. They have tried hard enough to make our people suffer.

Question: Since Chávez came to power, Venezuela has begun to vote in favor of Cuba in the UN Human Rights Commission (UNHRC).

You accuse the nations who vote against Cuba there of "submitting to US pressure." Why not say that the Venezuelan government has submitted itself to Havana?

Germán Sánchez: Quite the opposite. Venezuela has adopted the same position as many other governments in respecting Cuba's sovereignty and its right to apply its own laws.

It is the people of Venezuela who must judge the dignified and independent vote of the government of Venezuela. The votes of all the countries against that resolution—despite the brutal pressures to which they were subjected—represent more than 70 percent of the world's population, because India, Pakistan, China and South Africa were there, and there were 20 countries against.

Does the United States have the right to condemn Cuba in that commission? It is a country that has just failed to recognize the UN and that has committed the most brutal and flagrant violation of all human rights in Iraq. Is the United States in a position to talk of human rights when it has hundreds of prisoners in Guantánamo who have not been brought to trial and who are existing, uprooted from their native lands, in subhuman conditions? In that commission, the United States succeeded, with some difficulty, in obtaining a lukewarm vote against Cuba, due to the pressure and threats that it exerted. When those same governments vote in secret, the majority does so against the United States, as was the case in 2001, when it was not part of the commission.

Every year, the United States makes every effort to win that anti-Cuba resolution. Why? In order to justify the blockade and its policy of aggression. That is why it pressures and threatens certain governments of the poor countries. It makes them yield by force. In the end, after a close vote, we are proud and consider it a victory for the Cuban people. Despite everything, the United States did not succeed in condemning Cuba for applying the law against 75 mercenaries and for executing three terrorists. It was defeated on that count and only achieved the usual tepid resolution.

Question: The UNHRC has asked Cuba to receive one of its representatives. Why does the island refuse? Does it have something to hide?

Germán Sánchez: No, of course not. What Cuba will not allow is for an empire to utilize force, threats and pressure to subject it to monitoring. We cannot permit any interference in our internal affairs.

That vote in Geneva is no longer news, especially when that empire has just ignored the United Nations. What authority is left in that agency, when it was not even capable of criticizing or condemning the aggression against Iraq?

Every year, the United States assesses the violation of human rights in the rest of the world, but does not examine itself. In the United States, 60 percent of prisoners are blacks and Latinos, and every year more than 80 people are executed — including minors and people with mental disabilities. They are killing people in Iraq and Afghanistan and protecting Cuban terrorists. They pretend to be untouchable, the judges of human rights.

Cuba is open to a daily confirmation of the respect for human rights on our island. We don't have anything to hide. We have close to two million tourists who visit us, plus thousands of other foreigners who live in Cuba or travel to the island on an annual basis. In no other country are the human rights of all people respected so completely, from the right to employment, education, nutrition, health and culture, to the right to express ideas and to genuinely participate in the exercise of political, economic and social life, without social, religious, ethnic or any other kind of discrimination.

Cuba is a long way from being the hell that "the unruly and brutal monster that scorns us" — as Martí put it — is depicting in its propaganda. Of course, neither is it a paradise — what country is? But we are happy to compare out virtues and achievements with any other nation, despite the criminal blockade and aggression to which we have been subjected for close to half a century.

4. The Bolivarian revolution and the social missions

On December 31, 2002, I had a brief conversation with President Hugo Chávez in his office at Miraflores Palace. Just a few minutes before saying goodbye, with both of us still seated, he stated with his customary eloquence and complete confidence: "We have concluded an extremely difficult, dangerous year, during which we had the initiative on very few occasions. But, despite almost always hitting back from against the ropes, we won the battle. Today we have concluded this defensive phase. From tomorrow, we will initiate the new, offensive stage of the revolution."

Hugo Chávez's assertion was without nuance. More than just listening to his words, I observed his confident gestures and expression and noted his serene conviction, although it was clear he did not have a plan of action in mind to make that assertion a reality. I farewelled the president convinced he would know how to lead his people and triumph in the face of new threats. The lessons and the formidable victories against the fascist coup plot of April and the December oil strike were behind him. The year 2003 promised to be equally complex and decisive for the Bolivarian process. Securing immediate benefits for the people and completing the political defeat of the opposition and its foreign allies were urgent tasks.

In January 2003 the president and the Venezuelan government were still forced to devote their full attention to defeating the oil strike. But by February, offensive measures were beginning to be more evident: exchange controls were established, putting an end to the multimillion-dollar capital flight of the previous weeks and providing an effective and opportune antidote to the collapse of the economy, which had suffered the ravages of destabilization.

Without any doubt, after September 2001, US President Bush's policy toward Venezuela toughened: short-term US policy was to remove Chávez from power. The aggressive actions of the bloc of the Venezuelan bourgeoisie and oligarchy and the Bush administration largely prevented the Bolivarian government from implementing its social and economic programs to benefit the people. Nevertheless, a large proportion of poor people—more than 65 percent of the population—maintained their faith in Chávez and his promises, and continued to trust in the strength of the Bolivarian constitution, which had been approved in the referendum of December 15, 1999.

But how long could those poor people, greatly affected by the crisis, wait for a new political reality capable of generating genuine change in their lives?

The situation allowed no sitting back, not a minute could be lost: political timing is one of the most important variables at any historical juncture. And that is what it was, a crucial point when the existence of the revolutionary project was at stake.

The government had to make advances, starting from an unavoidable premise: as a consequence of opposition actions, Venezuela's GDP had dropped by more than 20 percent during 2002, unemployment had increased by almost 25 percent, real wages significantly declined, only a few thousand homes were built, and basic goods were beyond the reach of millions of people. Hunger, begging and violence were all on the increase. Despite the fact that resources allocated to education and health had doubled since 1999, setbacks or stagnation had settled in both sectors, after certain successes. The successes included the creation of 2,000 new-style Bolivarian schools, with full-day sessions and three meals a day for students; and the reduction in the infant mortality rate by nearly four points (from 22 to 18 per 1,000 live births). Nevertheless, illiteracy remained at the same level, the revolution was barely making itself felt in the rest of the education sector, and public health services could not be sustained.

It was essential to act quickly and create benefits within the reach of the largest possible number of poor people, to show them with concrete examples that the revolution they had mobilized and fought for in April, and ardently backed in December, had social and economic content in addition to political and moral strength. But, speaking honestly, an immediate economic leap was not possible: first because structures required slower policies and strategic planning; and second, because events between the end of 2001 and January 2003 had caused a significant recession. The only possible immediate action—which was taken—was to restore oil production and thus reestablish the financial resources indispensable for taking the social and economic offensive.

Furthermore, the revolution had to take the offensive in the political field. In spite of the two major setbacks it suffered in April and in December, the opposition's financial resources were virtually intact, and it had the support of the private media and encouragement and backing from President Bush. It was planning a new stage: getting rid of Chávez by means of a recall referendum, which could feasibly be set in motion at the end of 2003 or in early 2004. Their calculations could not have been more cynical: they planned to utilize widespread discontent among broad sectors of the population—dissatisfaction that was caused by the crisis generated by the opposition itself. Failing to get rid of Chávez by unconstitutional means, the counterrevolution decided to work within the framework of the constitution. This scenario was highly risky for Chávez, as a reasonable number of his less conscious followers were susceptible to manipulation, a fact confirmed by reliable opinion polls.

At that crossroads of tension and hope, doubt and affirmation, Barrio Adentro (Inside the Barrio, or Inside Marginal Neighborhoods) and the other social missions leapt into existence in the course of 2003. They have become the most significant, fundamental events of the Bolivarian revolution after the political gains in 1999 (the new constitution), 2000 (Chávez's reelection), and 2001 (the passing of basic laws like the land reform and hydrocarbon laws). These social programs are authentic Venezuelan initiatives, and are unprecedented in any other Latin American country — including Cuba, where exceptional advances in health and education took longer to organize — in terms of their reach, originality, daring, speed, and popular and military participation.

From March 2003 the social missions began to flow like fresh spring water and between July 1 and November of that year almost all of them were well established. President Chávez formulated the broader concept of the social missions while organizing the battle against illiteracy in May 2003. The question was: how to bring together and direct all the actors who could make the eradication of illiteracy in Venezuela a possibility in less than 18 months? The president identified two principal support bases: the forces of civil society most committed to the Bolivarian process, and the military, which could provide significant logistical backing. He decided not to hand over direction of the task to the traditional state bureaucracy, but incorporated what it had to offer that was most needed — for example, material resources and cadres. The task was then given to the social missions themselves, which operated without formalistic schemes and with a unified and dynamic approach — the result of the desire to achieve effective, rapid results. A large proportion of the population participated in the missions, and they developed greater and greater enthusiasm as advances became evident.

Mission Robinson (the literacy campaign) was the pioneer of the social missions—formally launched on July 1, 2003, after it was set up in May. There were two precedents to the missions in March and April, linked to what would later be christened Mission MERCAL (nutrition) and Barrio Adentro (health), the latter being the most famous and popular of all the missions.

In response to the shortage of foodstuffs caused by the December 2002 oil strike, President Hugo Chávez realized that the government needed to create a powerful system for the wholesale purchase of foodstuffs and their retail distribution at prices accessible to low-income earners. In March, a commercial network was established that, through thousands of retailers of different sizes, could sell essential products to people at lower prices than on the private market. So, within a short space of time, Mission MERCAL came into existence.

On April 16, 2003, the first 58 Cuban doctors who were to establish Barrio Adentro arrived in Caracas. At that point, the mission was in its embryonic, experimental form. The people who initially drew up the program could never have imagined what would happen subsequently. President Chávez, however, was planning a similar program but on a national scale. In May he met with the 58 Cuban doctors and the mayor of Caracas, Freddy Bernal, to redesign the project and transform it into practical action.

In May 2003, President Chávez also decided to ask Fidel Castro for support in utilizing the Cuban "Yes, I Can" teaching method to eradicate illiteracy in 12 months [which led to the development of Mission Robinson]. A pilot project was immediately organized and coordinated by the armed forces in Caracas, Aragua and Vargas, and was highly successful. On the same organizational basis, the Venezuelan president set up three new education missions in the second half of the year: education up to sixth grade, secondary education and university education.

An interesting aspect of the social missions is their identity. Chávez has not only been their principal architect, he has also assigned them their names, associating each mission with a famous Venezuelan patriot. Missions Robinson I (the literacy campaign) and II (sixth grade) became rapidly known by their name—the pseudonym used by Simón Bolívar's teacher, Simón Rodríguez. The name Barrio Adentro immediately caught on within the country and internationally, especially after the impact of the program in the hills of Caracas where most of the country's poor live. The names of other missions were similarly popular: Mission Ribas (secondary school education), named in honor of the youthful independence martyr José Félix Ribas; Mission Sucre, invoking Antonio José de Sucre, the grand marshal of Ayacucho; Mission MERCAL, the initials of the food markets; and Mission Vuelvan Caras, named after the historic victory of General Páez and his troops over the Spanish royalists.

The social missions were formally launched at public events presided over by President Chávez, on the following days:

- Mission Robinson I: July 1, 2003
- Mission Robinson II: October 28, 2003
- Mission Sucre: November 3, 2003
- Mission Ribas: November 17, 2003
- Mission Barrio Adentro: December 14, 2003
- Mission MERCAL: January 2004

Mission Vuelvan Caras (to generate employment and stimulate autonomous economic development through cooperatives), Mission Identidad (giving of identity cards to 5,076,660 Venezuelans and registering 1,232,000 on the voter lists), and

Mission Hábitat (designed to resolve the housing crisis in 10 years), likewise emerged in 2004.

These were the missions that came into existence in 2003 and 2004, which became the engine of the new stage of the Bolivarian revolution. They represent the principal dynamic factors that made the recent great Bolivarian victories possible: the recall referendum of August 15, 2004, and the regional elections of October 30, 2004, in which the revolution won 20 of the 22 states in dispute and more than 75 percent of the mayoralties.

The social missions emerged at a historic crossroads in the Bolivarian process, out of the search for genuine solutions to the grave social and economic problems of Venezuela's poor, who number more than 17 million out of the country's 25 million inhabitants.

They are based on a new relationship between the state and civil society and claim the broadest and most effective participation of the people in solving their own problems. The missions are at the center of the Bolivarian government's policy to combat poverty in a fundamental and decisive way. They are based on President Chávez's concept of granting power to the poor so they can become protagonists in their own emancipation and can gain more power and fortify their principal role in the defense, support and development of the Bolivarian revolution. In that sense, the social missions represent a decisive historical stage in the advance and consolidation of the Bolivarian process. The Bolivarian revolution has been able to crystallize its democratic and popular nature thanks to the social missions, and to a significant degree, its future development depends on their effectiveness.

The social missions are the direct beneficiaries of the new blueprint for distributing oil profits in a just way. They are not programs simply seeking short-term palliative solutions, and while they might continue to develop in the future, they are already achieving positive solutions for the poor.

State institutions are participating in their organization and leadership but the missions are not subordinated to traditional bureaucratic structures. Each mission has its own profile and a notable degree of creativity, its ultimate aim being to meet the human rights enshrined in the Bolivarian constitution. In the fields of health, education, housing, employment, nutrition, sports and culture, among others, the missions are run in such a way that they embody a primal force for fulfilling the 1999 constitution; they represent its raison d'être. They are aimed at transforming an inherited legacy, and at the same time, establishing new legal standards in tune with the imperatives of revolutionary change.

For President Chávez, "these social missions are the nucleus of the strategic offensive to progressively reduce poverty, to give power to the poor. That is their challenge, to solve old ills and simultaneously create the structural conditions to facilitate the construction of a new society, in which everyone will be members with equal rights and duties."

How will the social missions allow the poor to gain power?

Let us examine Barrio Adentro, Robinson I and II, Ribas, Sucre and MERCAL, to evaluate their strategic advances within the Bolivarian revolution.

Prior to Barrio Adentro, the health panorama in Venezuela was similar to that of other Latin American nations, with the exception of Cuba. More than 17 million Venezuelan people were excluded from general medical attention and wide sectors of the middle class were suffering—and still are—from the onslaught of the privatization and commercialization of health services.

The figure of 58 Cuban doctors who arrived in the poor barrios of Caracas in April 2003 quickly swelled in the following months, to the point where they were providing health care for all the poor citizens of Caracas. From July, the program was extended to the rest of Venezuela and between October and November alone more than 4,000 Cuban health professionals arrived. On December 14, 2003, when President Chávez formally announced the launch of Barrio Adentro, it had already expanded to almost every corner of the country, and was being carried out by 10,179 Cuban doctors, hundreds of nurses and some Venezuelan physicians.

The Venezuelan Medical Federation—a fanatical defender of the commercialization of health care—opposed from the outset this new, revolutionary and humanist mode of health care for the poor, and with the private media's full support unleashed a furious campaign against the Cuban doctors. The results of the doctors' work, however, and their willingness to live among the poor and attend to people on a 24-hour basis, in their homes, ensured the resounding failure of that campaign: the overwhelming majority of the population rejected it. Even political opposition leaders were seeking medical treatment from the Cuban doctors and refrained from criticizing such an altruistic mission.

Barrio Adentro is based on a concept of general health, combining both primary and preventive care, placing an emphasis on educating people and gaining their support in averting the causes of illnesses. This is made possible by doctors actually living in the communities and is supported by the work of local health committees, which have rapidly proliferated throughout the country. Barrio Adentro is linked with work around sports, nutrition, the environment, social economy, culture and education. It is important to note that the vast majority of the doctors began their work in improvised consulting rooms, either in the houses where they were living or nearby, and almost always in cramped and difficult conditions. In spite of the fact that the president assigned resources to build consulting rooms and fit them out with the necessary furniture and equipment, this did not occur quickly due to serious bureaucratic shortcomings. However, thanks to the generous and creative support of the population, practical solutions were found that have facilitated the doctors' daily labor.

One innovative aspect of this mission is the free dispensing of medicine to every patient attended by a doctor. The doctors have access to about 100 medicines with which they can treat about 95 percent of common ailments.

In this way, Barrio Adentro was meeting the preventive and primary care needs of 17 million people, with a total of approximately 14,000 doctors (one to every 250 families). Once this was accomplished, two new services were initiated. From late 2003 to mid-2004, free dental and eye care was established throughout the country, including ophthalmology services and the provision of free glasses and 3,019 dental and 459 optical chairs. These services similarly covered 17 million poor people. One outstanding aspect of the dental service is the incorporation of some 1,200 young Venezuelan professionals who work in an integrated, fraternal way with 3,000 Cuban colleagues and at the same time study with those Cubans to reach specialist level.

Barrio Adentro's next step was the installation of 84 diagnostic centers in the states of Miranda, Zulia, Carabobo, Táchira and Caracas. In September and October 2004, these centers began to offer free electrocardiographic, endoscopic, ultrasound, X-ray and laboratory services. In 2005 there are plans to extend these diagnostic services to all poor people throughout the country, likewise free of charge. Their results have been so successful that President Chávez has asked Cuba to provide these services to the middle class.

Not stopping there, in July 2004, in coordination with the Barrio Adentro doctors, one of the most noble, generous social programs ever conceived emerged: Mission Milagro (Miracle). Milagro guarantees free surgery in Cuba for all Venezuelans suffering from cataract and other eye disorders. The service includes transportation, board and lodging for the patients and covers the same costs for a companion, if needed. In less than six months, more than 20,000 people have had their sight restored. In 2005, another 100,000 patients with visual difficulties are to be treated. Describing it as a "miracle" has been no exaggeration.

Other interesting statistics confirm the efficiency and success of Barrio Adentro: on average, the Cuban doctors give 6.4 million consultations every month. They visit 1.22 million families, direct 3.9 million educational activities, and save close to 1,000 lives. Each month, Cuban and Venezuelan dental surgeons offer 720,000 consultations, do 680,000 fillings and 160,000 extractions, carry out 710,000 educational activities, and conduct 210,000 checks for mouth cancer. For their part, opticians examine an average of 188,000 people per month, also supplying glasses as required.

Significantly, under the Barrio Adentro program there were 76 million consultations in the year 2004 alone, while in the five-year period 1994–98 there were barely 70 million consultations within the entire Venezuelan public health system. Of course, beyond the statistics, the fundamental aspect of Barrio Adentro is the quality of the medical care, the fact that it is free, its preventive focus and the tremendous psychological security felt by people previously excluded who now have guaranteed access to a family doctor.

One valuable aspect of Barrio Adentro concerned those patients for whom further diagnosis was necessary. On many occasions patients could not afford this and never received further tests, as diagnostic services in the public sector are inadequate or nonexistent.

Positive trials in the 84 initial diagnostic centers confirmed the need to offer these services to everyone within the Barrio Adentro program. Furthermore, President Chávez decided to extend these services to the country as a whole, offering them to everyone. That concept of universal access gave rise to another daring, exceptional idea: the creation of a secondary health system not just in diagnostics but in intensive care and emergency services, capable of saving the lives of 100,000 people every year; and the establishment of another secondary health system for rehabilitation and physiotherapy. Both would have nationwide coverage.

President Chávez christened the new combination of services Barrio Adentro II and took advantage of his annual speech to the National Assembly to announce it, indicating that it would be fully in place by March 2005.

When I heard the details of this huge leap into the future, I couldn't help but exclaim: "It sounds like science fiction!" Yet, under the personal direction of the president, intensive work is already underway on the project, with close coordination between Cuban doctors, other specialists and diverse Venezuelan institutions.

Barrio Adentro II will very soon become a reality, transcending Venezuela's borders to become an example of what an excellent health system—free to everyone—could and should be.

Barrio Adentro II includes:

- 600 general diagnostic centers (CDIs) with 24-hour emergency and intensive care services, 150 of them with emergency operating theaters. They are able to provide X-ray, laboratory and ultrasound services; microanalytic systems to detect viral and congenital diseases; and endoscopic, electrocardiographic and ophthalmology facilities.

- 35 hi-tech diagnostic centers (one in each state and two or three in the larger states), with cutting-edge diagnostic equipment that, in conjunction with the CDIs, facilitates the accurate detection or diagnosis of most illnesses. Each center will have facilities for CAT scans, MRI scans, noninvasive ultrasound, video-endoscopy and mammography and floating X-ray units, among other services.

- 600 rehabilitation and physiotherapy rooms, with electrotherapy, thermotherapy, hydrotherapy, occupational therapy, natural and traditional medicine, podiatry, gymnasium facilities and services for speech and hearing disorders.

The impact of Barrio Adentro II on the Venezuelan public and private health systems remains to be seen. It is expected to have a positive influence within the public sector, prompting essential changes, and allowing hospitals to fulfill their important role, and to complete an excellent combination of health services based on general primary care.

One innovative and significant contribution of Barrio Adentro is the training of 40,000 Venezuelan doctors over the next 10 years. There will be direct links between students and doctors involved in the missions, both I and II.

It is an iconoclastic concept of education, and is a new way of training general community doctors with reliable professional and practical experience and in the essential ethics of serving people rather than using patients for personal gain.

Within this scheme, every Cuban doctor works with a small group of students. The students learn with audiovisual materials and in computer classes, and the Cuban physicians act as guides, facilitators and trainers in the consulting rooms, the Barrio Adentro II facilities, and in their daily contact with the population. At the same time, 5,000 students will be trained to university level as technicians, to handle the equipment in the diagnostic and rehabilitation centers.

In a few years, Venezuela will have enough doctors to replace their Cuban counterparts and will even be able to accompany the latter on other Barrio Adentro missions elsewhere in the Americas.

As an important component of Barrio Adentro, in April 2003 a group of Cuban professionals in sports and physical recreation began to work in the Libertador municipality of Caracas. For the first time in those barrios, many children, adults and senior citizens had the possibility of participating in sports, undertaking physical education, or organizing themselves to practice basic gymnastics, dance therapy, or other activities. The success of the program was so resounding that it was soon extended to the whole country and today these coaches are offering their services to anyone living in poor areas who is interested. There are currently 8,250 sports teachers in the mission, with a ratio of one to approximately 2,200 people. Like the doctors, these professionals live with people in the barrios, and with the support of the population, are making it possible for people to practice sports in open or covered areas. Each teacher works with one or two young Venezuelan sports workers and has close links with the Barrio Adentro doctors, who support them in rehabilitation treatment, developing exercise programs for pregnant women, and other similar tasks.

In summary, the program of sports, and a culture of physical recreation in the context of Barrio Adentro, has become an innovative way to improve the quality of life of millions of people.

When Hugo Chávez assumed the presidency in February 1999, the state of public education in Venezuela was horrific. The school attendance rate stood at just 59 percent, there were 1.5 million illiterates, more than two million adults who had only reached sixth grade, and close to a further two million who had been unable to complete their secondary education. The situation was compounded by the more than 500,000 secondary school graduates who could not find a place at the universities, which had virtually become the preserve of students from private schools. The quality of teaching was steadily deteriorating and the education budget was at barely 2.8 percent of GDP.

The revolutionary government adopted very important measures during 1999–2001: it created 2,000 Bolivarian schools with full-day sessions, increased the education budget to more than 5 percent of GDP, and prohibited enrollment charges in public schools. Excluded children began to be incorporated into the education system. Teachers' salaries were raised and their work recognized as truly important.

The major transformation of the education system, however, occurred in 2003 with Missions Robinson I and II, Mission Ribas and Mission Sucre.

These Venezuelan educational missions represent a landmark in Latin American and Caribbean educational policies. Each mission has in common the use of audiovisual teaching aids and the central role of facilitators. Facilitators serve as mediators between video classes that are prerecorded by excellent teachers and the students, who watch and participate in those lessons together. This method has worked successfully in all the educational missions; it guarantees the homogeneity of each course as well as high-quality educational content that is both attractive and accessible to the average student. It has been demonstrated at all levels of education that the critical mass of knowledge acquired by the students is very high, due in large part to the video classes that provide explanations and information.

Mission Robinson was the pioneer in this new educational concept. A pilot project was run in May–June 2003, which demonstrated the effectiveness of the Cuban literacy method "Yes, I Can." Based on 65 audiovisual classes, the course makes it possible for illiterate students to learn to read and write in seven weeks. In May, President Chávez formed the national Presidential Literacy Commission, and other groups at the state and municipal levels composed of officials from the ministries of Education, Culture, and Energy and Mines; officers from the armed forces; managers of PDVSA; and governors and mayors. The commissions were bound to act with the backing of grassroots popular organizations.

On July 1 Mission Robinson was launched, which covered urban barrios and the plains, jungle and mountains. Hundreds of thousands of patriots (as the students were called) joined the project and in December of that year it was announced that one million Venezuelans had achieved literacy. The mission was virtually completed by the end of 2004. The mission's success entailed organizing 78,957 study areas nationally, with 80,000 televisions and video players, plus more than 100,000 facilitators and supervisors — civilian and military — who received a monthly wage equivalent to $100 for transportation and food costs.

This noble labor of love and culture was carried out with great joy and popular participation. Chávez's aim to give power to the poor through knowledge was put into practice. Poor people, even those who previously had the least access to education, immediately joined up and proved the validity of the idea. The literacy teachers, many of them young people or housewives, benefited from their diverse experiences and the moral and spiritual gains, and also acquired a fuller comprehension of the revolutionary process.

Various obstacles arose. The televisions, videos, cassettes, readers, notebooks and pencils had to be distributed over almost one million square kilometers. The armed forces guaranteed the success of this extraordinary logistical challenge, providing land, air and river transportation and access to army storerooms. Without that assistance, it would have been impossible to carry out the mission.

During the pilot study in May, it became clear that many pupils could not see the texts, and a program of eye tests for all those with problems was quickly instigated, which resulted in giving glasses to 300,000 people. When students abandoned their classes for various reasons, they were visited at home and persuaded to rejoin. All those who graduated were given a family library of 25 books. The most outstanding students received encouragement in the form of credits, housing and jobs.

Mission Robinson signified the unleashing of hope and potential. A 68-year-old woman affirmed emotionally to President Chávez during the graduation ceremony: "I thought of that saying 'you can't teach an old parrot how to talk,' but these classes are a miracle!" She was referring to the Cuban "Yes, I Can!" teaching method, which was made significantly Venezuelan. Through Mission Robinson, the method demonstrated that it is indeed possible to incorporate poor people into the educational revolution and represented an unprecedented explosion of motivation and participation, which would continue to grow with the other educational missions, through which the most excluded could reaffirm that, in fact, they could advance toward the light of knowledge.

Even before Mission Robinson started, an education program had been conceived to ensure that those who had learned to read and write, and other adults whose education ended before sixth grade, could reach that level. It also used audiovisual materials and relied on the guidance of facilitators. The "Yes, I Can Go On" teaching method emerged from the experiences of the application in Venezuela of the "Yes, I Can" method, and guarantees sixth-grade education in two consecutive years of study, including English and computer studies.

Mission Robinson II was formally launched on October 28, 2003, and within a few months had an intake of 1.2 million pupils, more than 60 percent of them recently literate.

This new mission, aimed at making it possible for more than one million adults to complete secondary school education, was similarly a great success. Within a few weeks of its inauguration on November 17, 2003, more than 800,000 people had joined the project. This time the logistical support, organization and direction of the mission was assigned to the Ministry of Energy and Mines and the state oil company PDVSA, as confirmation of their new role in serving the interests of the people. That decision also encouraged a greater ethical and political commitment to the Bolivarian process on the part of officials and workers at PDVSA.

The new mission adopted audiovisual teaching methods, and was similarly based on a close and fruitful cooperation between Venezuelan and Cuban specialists. They organized a system of education in the areas of science, humanities and technology to guarantee school-leaving certificates in just two years.

One Sunday, a survey was organized to take place in all the country's public plazas — which filled to overflowing — to discover the approximate number of school leavers without university places. The result: more than half a million people. In order to incorporate such a large number of school leavers into higher education, the decision was made to move forward in stages and in groups. Prior to entering university, each group would undertake a preparatory course aimed at refreshing and consolidating students' knowledge.

One fundamental aspect of Mission Sucre is the concept of the regionalization of higher education: in other words, to create university courses where students are living, and to create courses in line with the needs of each region and the country. It presupposes a departure from the narrow confines of university education — where classes are given in historic buildings and led by professors. That setup is replaced with more modest premises, video classes, and professional facilitators who are trained in this context.

A few months before that Sunday, on July 30, President Chávez announced plans for Mission Sucre and the regionalization of universities. On the same day, he inaugurated the first head-quarters of the Bolivarian University in the luxurious former offices of the oil technocrats and servants of the oligarchy and foreign capital—where studies in legal science, history and communications are now taking place.

One of the most innovative and striking attributes of the educational missions is the creation of 400,000 scholarships for the poorest students: 200,000 within Robinson II and 100,000 each within Ribas and Sucre. These scholarships consist of grants equivalent to $100 per month (70 percent of the minimum wage) and represent encouragement and real support, providing basic conditions so that recipients can undertake their studies. They also represent a genuine reduction in unemployment.

The embryo of the next great program dates back to the mass distress at the shortages caused by the oil strike of December 2002 and January 2003. At that time, President Chávez decided to instigate a vast, state-run entrepreneurial system to eliminate hunger and contribute to the improved nutrition of Venezuela's poor.

Today, Mission MERCAL—finally launched in January 2004—is a palpable reality. It benefits more than 10 million people with subsidized foodstuffs (at an average of 25 percent below market prices), and provides free food to those with no resources. The commercial establishments of the MERCAL network are everywhere. Food kitchens have been organized in the poor barrios, each offering free lunches and afternoon snacks to about 150 people, benefiting more than 900,000 people across the country and increasing this year to cover more than one million.

There is the extraordinary idea of converting these food kitchens into places where, in addition to food, people can receive health and educational attention and join in recreational, cultural, and sporting activities. That work is being undertaken with the support of the young members of the Francisco de Miranda Social Workers Front, who under the guidance of President Chávez are working cooperatively and methodically within all the country's poor barrios.

There is also the maximum security program that grants a 50 percent subsidy toward the price of seven essential items, currently benefiting two million people.

It is a fact that a food program of such reach has never previously been organized in any Latin American country. Mission MERCAL is a reference point of much interest to other countries, because it demonstrates the feasibility of counteracting the disastrous effects of neoliberalism, and demonstrates the proper role of governments in the distribution of wealth, if those governments really are committed to producing democratic and sovereign nations.

In summary, MERCAL is making a tremendous contribution to the immediate problems of hunger and malnutrition. Moreover, thanks to the existence of the other social and economic programs with which it interacts, it is developing with a broad perspective.

Cuban participation in Barrio Adentro and the educational missions

The following questions and responses have been drawn from several interviews conducted with the author between June 2003 and April 2005.

Question: Are the Cuban doctors participating in Barrio Adentro really physicians, or have they just come here to indoctrinate our people?

Germán Sánchez: Your question is opportune, because it allows me to refer to one of the most widespread lies in relation to the Cuban doctors who are offering their services in the poor barrios of Caracas. Ever since the arrival in 1999 of the first Cuban health contingent, to help people affected by the landslide in Vargas, members of the Venezuelan Medical Federation and other spokespeople for similarly questionable causes have charged our doctors at best with being untrained professionals arriving to take jobs away from Venezuelan doctors, and at worst, with being undercover agents. They said then — and are reiterating this now — that the real role of the Cuban doctors was to politicize people in favor of President Chávez. It was slanderous then — in the face of a natural disaster — and is now, in the face of the social disaster the Cuban doctors have come to confront.

With respect, I would suggest that your question should be answered by the 17 million citizens who have benefited from the thorough, daily work — at any hour — of our doctors, all of whom are highly qualified and educated with the philosophy to serve human beings rather than profit from them. The first thing those humble Venezuelans say is that nobody can ever take that medical attention away from them. Our doctors are contributing to combating the horrendous conditions of those communities, which are weighed down with problems and inequalities, but at the same time are rich with humanism and the capacity to welcome anyone who has decided to offer them solidarity and aid without deception.

No Cuban doctor will ever become involved in Venezuelan politics. Their work is strictly professional. Naturally, they bring with them the values and ideas of our people. I ask myself: Are the schemers afraid of the Venezuelan people's access to these opinions? As Cubans, we are confident of our historical direction and whether in Cuba or in any corner of the planet we are disposed to talk about our social realities.

Question: Why is Cuba sending so many doctors to Venezuela? Wouldn't it be better if they remain on the island, where there are huge health problems?

Germán Sánchez: The presence of Cuban doctors in Bolívar's homeland is nothing out of the ordinary. Firstly, we are paying a historical debt of gratitude to the first nation that taught us the course of freedom and independence, and which has always acted in solidarity with us. Cuba has close to 70,000 doctors, one for every 160 people, the highest ratio in the world. For years now, our physicians have been lending their services in many countries, in places where medical attention is not available and where governments have requested our help. Prior to the Barrio Adentro experience more than 53,000 Cuban health professionals and technicians worked in 93 countries. At present, not counting Venezuela, approximately 4,000 Cuban doctors are working in 22 countries, and have saved the lives of more than 461,000 people. More than 500 Cuban health workers are offering their services in countries such as Guatemala and Haiti. In all those places, they work voluntarily and with altruism, without receiving a salary from their host nation, and those governments do not pay Cuba any fees. Our country guarantees their salaries and takes responsibility for the quality and ethics of their work. They respect the customs and laws of those nations. No other country in the world trains doctors in the vocation of solidarity and it is a matter of pride and satisfaction for our health professionals to help other peoples who are suffering great hardship.

In relation to the Cuban health service, it makes more sense to talk figures: average life expectancy is 77 years, the infant mortality rate is 5.8 per 1,000 live births. The entire population has access to free preventive attention and high-quality care. No one in Cuba is suffering or dying from lack of medical attention. All citizens are given several vaccinations; our country manufactures 70 percent of the medicines it consumes and some of its own hi-tech equipment; thousands of scientists are researching cancer, HIV/AIDS, and developing new vaccines and cutting-edge medicines; illnesses such as polio, diphtheria, tetanus, measles, German measles, meningitis, mumps, hemophilia and hepatitis have been eradicated or controlled. We are producing vaccines against meningitis, hepatitis B, leprosy, tetanus and diphtheria, among others. Currently, research trials of vaccines against cholera (which does not exist on the island), tuberculosis and other strains of hepatitis and meningitis are underway, as well as pneumonia and Alzheimer's disease. We have more than 2,500 scientists working in human health research, and they are supported by advanced scientific and technological resources.

Suffice to say, for example, that European and US companies have 52 projects for developing anticancer vaccines and Cuba — alone — has nine, four of them at the stage of clinical trials. Moreover, we are advancing on various congenital disease programs: in 1982 we were the second country in the world to have a diagnostic and prenatal prevention plan for congenital malformations, and cretinism was eliminated in 1986, thanks to the congenital hypo-thyroid program. Our scientists have invented technology that can detect and measure auditory problems before children are born.

In summary, the Cuban health strategy combines both an efficient system of primary care centered on family doctors, with the use of the latest technologies, medicines and vaccines. It is sustained by excellent scientific research and a developed pharmaceutical industry.

Between these two extremes, we have 267 hospitals and 444 polyclinics, which are currently being renovated and improved. Cuba will soon be the country with the finest and most modern health system in the world, for all citizens. This advance in our health services means we expect to achieve an average life expectancy of 80 within five years.

Question: How many doctors is Cuba thinking of sending to Venezuela?

Germán Sánchez: Our commitment is to cover the primary care needs of all poor families at the ratio of one doctor to 1,200 citizens. There are currently some 14,000 general physicians and just over 3,000 dentists.

Cuba has many more doctors ready to fulfill this noble and historic mission in any part of Venezuela. All of them are specialists in general medicine and have an average experience of more than 10 years. This semester [in 2005] a further 6,000 new doctors, technical personnel and other professionals are to begin work in the 600 diagnostic centers and rehabilitation centers and the 35 hi-tech diagnostic centers in Venezuela.

High-level training and professional experience complement the ethics and humanism of our doctors. No country in the world trains doctors with a double education in ethics and professionalism, doctors who are then capable of fulfilling their duty in any circumstances or location on the planet. That is what prompts amazement and admiration of our doctors. They are noted for their humility, dedication and satisfaction at having done their job. This is even more the case in Venezuela, because all the doctors know they are part of a unique experience in Latin America: for the first time, the poorest sectors of a country are receiving high-quality, comprehensive health care, and this will soon also be the case for the rest of the population.

Our intention is not to replace Venezuelan doctors, but the reverse; it is about collaborating to obtain accelerated results for the entire population; to drastically reduce morbidity and mortality rates. We are sure this experience will become a paradigm of worldwide interest and impact. Hopefully our doctors will soon begin to be replaced by their Venezuelan colleagues, and in the not too distant future, united efforts will help our sisters and brothers in Brazil, Ecuador, Colombia and other nations of Latin America. Cuba's commitment is to help train 40,000 Venezuela doctors within 10 years. The first 20,000 young students are about to start their community medical courses. A further 20,000 young

Venezuelans are to study medicine in Cuba, living throughout the country in the homes of Cuban families.

Question: What about malpractice by the Cuban doctors?

Germán Sánchez: In fact, the malpractice has been committed on the part of certain media and officials in health trade unions and institutions—it is they who have displayed a lack of ethics.

In all the cases of so-called bad practice that have been investigated and exposed, it has been irrefutably demonstrated that these were publicity stunts to discredit our doctors, to promote fear among the population, to encourage a public rejection of Barrio Adentro, and to cause the failure of the health program. These stunts were led by directors of professional institutions—like the Venezuelan Medical Federation—and [private] hospitals, which have lied to the Venezuelan people and displayed a total absence of professionalism toward their Cuban colleagues. It is significant that almost all the leaders of the political opposition parties have said very little and have not really joined in these campaigns. Is that because they are aware of the real impact of our doctors on millions of people? We have remained calm in the face of such insults, because the people have not let themselves be confused.

Question: Let's change the subject. I would like to know why Cuba selected Venezuela for the "Yes, I Can" literacy teaching method.

Germán Sánchez: It was the other way around. President Chávez was aware of the existence of this highly innovative method and asked Fidel to implement it in Venezuela. It all happened very quickly. Fidel first publicly described the method in his 2003 May Day speech. Then, in the first week of May, he personally presented Chávez with the course videos. Within 24 hours, Chávez had viewed the tapes and made the decision to organize a giant literacy campaign. He recognized the educational quality of the course and correctly perceived that it could be successfully adapted to Venezuelan realities. He quickly came up with the very Venezuelan name Mission Robinson, created the Presidential Literacy Commission and other leadership structures, and gave instructions to the armed forces to undertake a pilot scheme with 400 illiterate people. He also proposed the goal: to teach one million people to read and write by the end of the year and to eliminate illiteracy during 2004.

Of course, Fidel, the Cubans working on developing the new method, and all of us—the Cuban people—accepted President Chávez's appeal with great enthusiasm and considered it an honor.

Venezuela has exceptional conditions for the development of a literacy program of such magnitude. As far as I know, at the present time it could not be achieved in any other Latin American country, even one with similar geography and numbers of illiterate people. Why can it be achieved in Venezuela? First, because a process of widespread social work and a high degree of popular participation is developing here; second, because of the doctrine of the armed forces—the defense of sovereignty based on equality and social justice—and its experience of direct action to the benefit of communities, which dates back to 1999 [the Vargas landslide]; and third, the fact that the nation's president has the humanism and leadership to direct a civil-military mission of great magnitude and complexity. There are two further reasons: years of intense struggles have produced social leaders and thousands of people prepared to take on big responsibilities without any desire for personal gain; and due to various factors, the government's social agenda had fallen behind, so since 2003 President Chávez has been pushing it forward with great speed. We have no doubts: Venezuela is already the first country in the South to have succeeded in eradicating illiteracy in the first years of the 21st century. Moreover, it has done so in a very short period of time, converting Mission Robinson into a global benchmark and Venezuela into the second Latin American country free of illiteracy.

Question: Who guarantees the method's effectiveness?

Germán Sánchez: Mission Robinson has not only been successful in terms of the Cuban "Yes, I Can" method. Its educational quality is unquestionable. Its methodology is based on the relationship between numbers and letters; in other words, it is based on illiterate people's knowledge of numbers, and then advances toward learning letters, syllables and words. It is simple and rapid. Audiovisual material is made comprehensible and attractive. The video classes demonstrate a teacher working with a group of students — in reality, Cuban actors — who, in 65 half-hour classes, also using the primer, learn to write and write. The classes are animated and reinforced with images, attractive texts and commentaries on diverse themes. The real students, in groups of up to 10, watch each class and are guided by a facilitator. With two classes every day, students learn to read and write in seven weeks.

Cuba's authority in literacy work is nothing new. In 1961 our people eliminated illiteracy in eight months, using a traditional literacy manual and primer and utilizing the mass participation of young people who lived with those they were teaching. That experience was unprecedented and has not been repeated in other countries. Cuba became a paradigm for specialized literacy institutions and a source of inspiration and experience for other countries.

Out of a desire to help other peoples, our country recently developed a radio literacy teaching method, which has been successful in some of the countries where it has been applied; more than 300,000 people have learned to read and write in that way. The "Yes, I Can" method is the result of a secular experience and the sound foundation of our pedagogy, which has received five UNESCO awards for its contribution to literacy.

It is very important to highlight the adaptation of that method which has taken place in Venezuela. Various changes have already been made, such as in the ratio of pupils to facilitators, and in the guiding and complementary role of the latter. One tremendous example of the creativity of the Venezuelan teachers is the application of the Cuban method to Braille language for the blind.

"Yes, I Can" possesses undeniable merits, but we should recognize that its success in Venezuela is a consequence of the responsible, enthusiastic and widely participatory manner in which it has been implemented and adapted, with a clear Venezuelan imprint.

Question: In real terms, how many literacy teachers did Cuba send?

Germán Sánchez: When President Chávez mentioned that Mission Robinson was to use a Cuban teaching method, it was as if he stepped on a nest of snakes. I heard on radio, saw on television, and read in newspapers so many malicious comments and twisted speculations that I felt it would be wise not to make any statement and to wait until the facts could speak for themselves. And that's how it was. Those who argued about the presence of thousands of Cuban literacy teachers, about indoctrination, who said that Cuba had no contribution to make in the field of literacy, and other nonsense, were soon silenced. The results are irrefutable. Will they learn their lesson? Will they finally realize that Cuba is not the hell they paint it to be, or the backwater they attempt to make it seem in order to frighten and confuse the naive? Will they need a special Mission Robinson to teach them literacy in ethics and professionalism?

Our human contribution to Mission Robinson has been what

Venezuela requested: three advisors for each state and 11 at the national level, all highly qualified individuals who feel a strong spirit of cooperation. Other assistance, on Fidel's initiative, has been to provide a significant proportion of the mission's technical base: televisions, video recorders, readers, facilitator manuals, cassettes of recorded classes, prescription glasses and ophthalmic equipment with the relevant technical personnel. As Cubans we feel proud to know that our contribution will result in one of the most significant events in the history of education in Venezuela and the world.

Question: Is Cuba to continue supporting Venezuela in Mission Robinson II (sixth grade) and in other education programs like Missions Sucre and Ribas?

Germán Sánchez: Yes, we are prepared to do that. Venezuelan-Cuban coordination in Mission Robinson has been a complete success and that gives us an even greater commitment to the Venezuelan people to work on other educational projects of similar reach with the country's educators. Moreover, we feel that this Venezuelan-Cuban educational alliance, based on mutual respect for the identity and decisions of both nations, will have repercussions in other places; furthermore, our specialists are also learning a tremendous amount here. Together we can extend our bilateral experiences to help other Latin American and Caribbean countries.

Cuban and Venezuelan educators have agreed on the content of the programs and the method of recording classes for both the first to fourth grade course and the fifth to sixth grade course. Cuban teachers recorded six classes for use in any country, while their Venezuelan counterparts recorded the geography and history classes. The course takes students up to sixth grade using the same technical materials (television, video tapes) as Mission Robinson, and facilitators guided by adult education teachers—

all Venezuelan—to guarantee the educational direction. Cuba is advising a group of assessors and the classes are recorded, edited and reproduced on the island.

Similarly, we are collaborating with Missions Ribas and Sucre, providing advisors and logistical support. Since the 1960s, Cuba has been developing the concept of the universalization of higher education and has created the conditions for all school leavers to have access to university studies, based on a national education system that extends throughout the island, and through an extensive scholarship network.

Within that framework, a new system has been developed in recent years: the regionalization of higher education, which allows all school leavers access to university careers. This idea goes beyond the training of professionals to meet the demands of the economy. At the center of the regionalization of university is the cultural and educational advancement of individuals, and in the final analysis, of the people as a whole. That unique Cuban experience has been placed at the disposal of Venezuela, which has distinct realities in terms of the huge number of school leavers without access to higher education, and its particular labor requirements.

In relation to Mission Sucre and the Bolivarian University, our country has opened up its experience in the regionalization of higher education. Venezuela has been able to adapt it to its own circumstances and is giving it a lot of support. Reaching the level we have reached took us 40 years. Venezuela can achieve it much sooner, thanks to the organizational precedent and the mass experience of recorded courses contributed by Missions Robinson I and II.

With Missions Robinson, Ribas and Sucre, Plan Simoncito (kindergarten) and the Bolivarian schools, Venezuela is placing itself in the vanguard of profound educational changes for the peoples of Latin America. It is a great source of joy for Cuba to humbly and efficiently accompany Venezuela in its magnificent liberationist Bolivarian project. As President Chávez understands, the foremost power of the people is knowledge.

Bolívar asked that morality and enlightenment transform our peoples. José Martí expressed it another way: "To be educated is the only way to be free." From Cuba we see clearly that Venezuela is advancing like never before towards freedom.

5. In the shadow of fascism

Cubans are independent, moderate and proud. They are masters of themselves and do not want other masters. Anyone who attempts to saddle them will be shaken off.

—José Martí

A chronicle of the attack on the Cuban embassy during the 2002 coup in Venezuela

April 9, 2002

That Tuesday, our embassy was functioning with apparent normality. It was not difficult to see that one sector of the opposition was trying to create a favorable opportunity to hit out at the constitutional government. Thus, we were aware of the dangerous and complex situation that was beginning to develop.

We were not surprised when, at 7:30 p.m. in the little PDVSA-Chuao Plaza, during a meeting televised by all the commercial TV channels, a woman by the name of Ruth Capriles who claimed to be the president of a "lookout" organization, shouted: "I have just been informed that people with black bags full of weapons have been leaving the Cuban embassy since this afternoon!"

I was at home with my wife and son when I suddenly saw and heard that madwoman on television. Her statements revealed a new facet of the plot: utilization of the pretext of Cuba's supposed armed intervention as a means of justifying the criminal use of weapons against the people.

"Quick, to the embassy!" I said to the driver. With the car already in motion, I added: "Ruth Capriles's statements show that there is a plot involving the use of weapons, in which they are trying to involve us, and we have to be prepared for any eventuality."

On the way I decided to dictate a press statement to one of the officials at the embassy over my cell phone. We immediately sent it to some TV channels and radio stations, in order to refute what we considered to be a premeditated attempt to provoke a conflict and generate violence.

Events went into overdrive. Minutes later, certain persons began to engage in hostile acts against the embassy. They yelled out insults from cars and motorbikes while driving by the embassy at high speed, while passersby shouted insults going to or returning from the opposition meeting in PDVSA-Chuao, which was still taking place barely 800 meters from our headquarters.

More serious attacks began to occur at 10:00 p.m., suggesting what might follow. A Molotov cocktail was thrown from a car and exploded in the main door of the embassy. After a while, two tires were placed at the car park entrance and set on fire. A few minutes later, we heard gunfire in the streets. Within minutes, in response to an alarm call we made to the authorities, two DISIP [Venezuelan secret police] cars cruised the area and the disturbances stopped.

April 10, 2002

Barely 20 hours later, late Wednesday afternoon, when Carlos Ortega and Pedro Carmona announced an indefinite strike, we were certain that a reactionary coup would take place within the next 48 hours. We wasted no time; I called together the members of the embassy and gave them their instructions. We prepared ourselves for the worst. If the coup was successful, we knew we would be attacked with incalculable consequences, because wherever fascism has taken over—as in Pinochet's Chile and Videla's Argentina—Cubans have been the victims of assaults, kidnappings and murders. At that moment of high tension our team resembled a beehive, everyone going about their tasks with cooperation and cohesion.

As a result, the events that began at midnight on April 11 did not take us by surprise. The day before the coup several small groups attacked the embassy, the consulate and the residence with stones and bottles and increasingly shouted offensive slogans. Our embassy was a gauge measuring the tension of events. By dawn on the day of the coup the organizers had managed to create the ideologically and emotionally poisoned atmosphere necessary for mobilizing a sector of the population to attack the government.

April 11, 2002

In the morning I checked out the area from San Román to Chuao, in the east of Caracas. I noticed thousands of white people, including children and the elderly, marching in families and groups of friends with happy faces, many in fashionable clothing and almost all of them shouting in chorus: "He's going! He's going! He's going! Today's the day! Today's the day!" I commented to my wife: "It's an open secret, today is the day of the coup." This was confirmed when I heard nearby the roar of the hysterical crowd in PDVSA-Chuao, when Carlos Ortega and others directed them to Miraflores Palace.

As the coup unfolded, calm reigned outside our buildings, like the calm before the arrival of a Caribbean hurricane. All the Cubans—children, women and men—felt capable of standing up to any adversity. In those moments of uncertainty, the most accurate source of information we had was the television. While the protestors advanced on Miraflores Palace, outside the palace and in the neighboring streets we saw thousands of citizens ready to defend — with their lives — the integrity of President Chávez and his constitutional government.

Suddenly, I saw the first images of several people felled by bullets. I looked at my watch; it was a little after 3:00 p.m. Again and again the television replayed that macabre footage and accused the president of the crimes. Afterwards, the military forces involved in the coup went into action, and one after the other, made their traitorous and anti-constitutional statements. Around midnight, news from our friends inside the palace of the imprisonment of President Chávez in Tiuna Fortress confirmed the consummation of the coup.

Once the military coup was concluded, and as the night progressed, small groups of people began to attack our cars parked in the street, spraying threats and anti-Cuban slogans on them. Some people punctured the tires and damaged the bodywork. We also heard a lot of aggressive shouting. Meanwhile, outside our residence in San Román, there were constant threats. Dead on midnight, several cars and a motorbike with two individuals stopped outside the house; those on the bike, both with guns in their hands, tried to enter the residence, but fled immediately on being detected from the first-floor balcony by one of our compañeros, Rafael Hidalgo.

We were no longer in any doubt. The crimes committed by the masterminds of the coup, the unscrupulous means they used to convince thousands of people that they were acting in a peaceful and democratic manner, and the state of fanaticism and confusion generated by the media campaigns in the eastern sector of the city, suggested that they would shortly act in the same manner against our embassy.

April 12, 2002

At 8:00 a.m. on April 12 — barely four hours after President Hugo Chávez was taken to the Tiuna Fortress — a known Cuban terrorist phoned the embassy, giving his name, Salvador Romaní, and saying he was on his way "with a group of people to take over the embassy." Thus the fascist plot against Cuba began, perfectly synchronized and coordinated by Romaní's chiefs in Miami and their counterparts in Venezuela.

I instructed an official to inform the Baruta police by phone and to ask for Romaní's immediate detention. We also called Mayor Capriles Radonski, but were informed that he could not be located, so we left him a message. Nobody responded.

Our compañero spoke with Commissioner Osvaldo García, chief of operations, who said he would respond within 10 minutes, but failed to do so. We insisted again and García then confirmed that a police detachment was on its way to protect the embassy. We were suitably surprised to discover that this was just two police officers.

At 8:30 a.m. Ricardo Koesling, another known terrorist, appeared at the main entrance to the embassy. Demonstrating his support for the coup, this Venezuelan lawyer, linked to the worst crimes and in the pay of the Miami Cuban-American mafia, arrogantly told one of our embassy officials that a large number of people were on their way to seize the embassy, because of the presence in the embassy of Diosdado Cabello, vice-president of the government, and other leaders. He also mentioned the alleged distribution of weapons by the embassy.

From that point, in an orchestrated manner, various media organizations repeated the same infamies. Meanwhile, the two Baruta police officers, with their arms folded, listened impassively to those lies and acted with the same passivity when dozens of people began to arrive to add to the rapidly escalating assaults.

One of them asked the other: "What do you reckon is going to happen here?" The response was a facial gesture of profound concern.

By 11:00 a.m. the size of the mob had grown to more than 1,000 people, thanks to the efforts of Koesling, Romaní and other Cuban and Venezuelan fascists, backed by several of the country's large media organizations. The inflamed mob unleashed its fury and malice. Before midday the electricity and water supplies to the embassy and consulate were cut off. The television cameras filmed these acts of violence and captured the shouts and hate-distorted faces. Everything was recorded in images and sound and then relayed by television channels in Venezuela and throughout the world. "They're going to have to invent plastic food!" Salvador Romaní proclaimed with unusual relish. Meanwhile another fascist, the youthful Juan Cristóbal Romero Iribarren, said: "They're going to have to eat the carpets, chairs and tables... because no food is going in, no water is going in... we're going to cut off their power...!"

I was talking to [Cuban] Foreign Minister Felipe Pérez Roque when the power was cut off. I said to him: "Now we have no water or electricity, from now on anything could happen." I added: "We're ready for anything."

I went out into the passage outside my office and observed one of the children helping his mother carry sacks full of papers to be burned. In the face of such imminent danger, the Cuban children who were with us in the embassy and the residence were both our greatest pain and our most beautiful pride. I went to the other offices, reviewing the positions of each compañero and all their calm and conscious activity. Nobody was overexcited, despite the fact that we hadn't slept for three or four nights and that we were terribly concerned that President Hugo Chávez might be assassinated, and an exceptional historical opportunity frustrated in Venezuela.

Some hours earlier, at dawn, Chávez had rung me from his office in Miraflores to tell me of a recent phone call with Fidel, and to say that he would never forget Fidel's words of solidarity and encouragement. The coup leaders had already given him their ultimatum, but he did not feel defeated. His voice, gruff and affected by intense emotion, maintained the strength of his convictions.

The new circumstances of the assault on the embassy now obliged us to focus on our own defense and to preserve—on our diplomatic territory—the honor of our homeland. I went up to the top floor, and from a well-protected window furtively peeped out onto the street. The sun was at its highest and the suffocating heat was not diminishing the crowd's wild fanaticism.

Salvador Romaní and Ricardo Koesling took part in everything. They also contemplated with smiles on their faces the people, at their instigation, destroying our cars. One person smashed through the windscreen of a car, reemerging in a state of ecstasy; a woman furiously hit another vehicle with a Venezuelan flag; a third individual hurled himself against the embassy door; and several people threw stones and car parts into the embassy or painted slogans. In the fascist minds of those individuals the moment had arrived to remove the "fig leaves" that they used while the democracy of the Fifth Republic existed.

Significantly, a few hours before reading the Pinochet-style decree in Miraflores, at the height of his arrogance, Romaní announced on television—from outside the Cuban embassy—the decision that Carmona subsequently signed: to dissolve all civil powers. It was not mere coincidence, but unequivocal evidence that those leading the siege and assault on the Cuban diplomatic mission were acting under the guidance of the coup plotters.

After 1:30 p.m. the frenzy reached its most critical and dangerous point. The euphoria and rancor of the demonstrators became more irrational under the effect of the leaders, and in many cases drugs and alcohol as well.

Meanwhile, they constantly yelled out slogans: "We're going in," "Not one step back," "We'll drag them out in handcuffs," "Murderers," "Get Diosdado out," "Not a drop more oil for Cuba," "Cubans out of Venezuela!" The most daring beat on the door in an attempt to break in. At the same time a group of terrorists attempted to take over an empty house behind the embassy with the aim of setting fire to the headquarters, after our neighbors on both sides had refused them access to their patios from where they planned to hurl Molotov cocktails at the embassy walls. That was the other macabre plan: to burn down the embassy and everyone inside it, including women and children. Some police officers, filmed by television cameras recording the Dantesque spectacle, managed to detain those people.

The bitter reality of that mob violence contrasted strongly with the demonstrators' supposed intention of defending "freedom and democracy." Those individuals boasting of being honorable members of civil society and sponsors of peaceful protest demonstrated in their frenzied trance their real face.

Those dishonorable images by which Venezuelan fascism revealed itself will go down in history.

As soon as footage from outside the embassy was shown on television, our telephones began constantly ringing with calls from friends and others who demonstrated their solidarity by offering to come down to repel the aggressors. In every case, we thanked the people for their gestures and asked them to avoid any confrontation. At the same time, we informed various public figures who called us, and others whom we contacted, of the aggression to which we were being subjected and the danger of an assault on us. Our officials spoke to a few hundred people by phone: ambassadors; authorities from the Baruta and City councils; foreign news and television agencies; Venezuelan human rights agencies; businesspeople; Monsignor Baltazar Porras, president of the Episcopal Conference, and other religious figures;

UN authorities; political leaders; certain military chiefs; cultural figures and national press editors; and the governor of Miranda. In addition, at 7:00 p.m. our official Amarilys Hernández spoke on the phone with the dictator Pedro Carmona and ordered him to find an immediate solution to the aggression on our headquarters.

The situation was becoming more complicated by the minute. Over a loudspeaker we heard the voices of the aggressors, giving us one hour to open the door and let the mob in, after which they would enter by force. I looked at my watch: it was a little after 3:00 in the afternoon. That ultimatum further inflamed the fanatics, who repeated the new threat: "We're coming in! We're coming in!"

Inside the embassy we continued with the tasks of surveillance and preparations to repel any aggression within the building. Every compañero, women and men, had a clearly defined task. We were firm, with our nerves on edge but ready to act—including at the cost of our lives—to prevent the sovereignty of our homeland from being violated. We maintained constant communication with the leadership of the [Cuban Communist] party and [Cuban] government; particularly with Fidel and Foreign Minister Felipe Pérez Roque. Our president was guiding us throughout. His words and constant interest in all the details of our situation heartened us and strengthened our convictions.

When I heard the ultimatum from the top floor of the embassy, I began a round of all the places guarded by our various compañeros. I gave them all final directions and the order to be ready to defend ourselves from attack, because we were not going to open our doors or make any concessions.

We could only partially observe what was happening in the street and the surrounding area. Our cameras had been displaced and then disabled by the power failure, and a wall prevented us from seeing some external movements, although friends gave us information over their cell phones. We did not respond even verbally to the aggression. From the windows we discreetly watched the mob and felt pity for those who were being incited to act without a full understanding of what they were doing.

Without wasting any time, I checked my compañeros' positions, and moving from one to another, we said our goodbyes, adding: *"Patria o muerte!"* (Homeland or death!) and *"Venceremos!"* (We will win!).

I went down to the ground floor. Descending the stairs the verses of our national anthem suddenly came from my soul. Everyone accompanied me from their position and that was the only time that our raised voices were heard:

Bayameses, forward to battle
the homeland contemplates you with pride
do not fear a glorious death
for to die for the homeland is to live!

To my surprise, when I reached the lobby to go over some final details with the compañeros on guard a few meters from the main door, I heard voices from the street calling for dialogue, saying that they were pacifists and did not want weapons to be used. Over a loudspeaker they informed us — with apparent seriousness — that the coup general, Damiani Bustillo, was there, as well as officials from the Baruta and City councils. They were urging dialogue. I listened attentively, trying to understand what was going on outside. At that moment I thought: "We are facing a classic scenario: first the use of force, then an ultimatum, and now proposed talks." I told the two compañeros who were guarding the main door: "Don't move and be on your guard, this could be a maneuver to take us by surprise."

I thought about our options for a few seconds and realized that although we had no guarantee that their intentions were genuine, we should pursue the slightest possibility of preventing a tragedy.

Thus I decided to ask for Fidel's authorization to proceed with negotiations. With his wisdom and experience, he formulated by phone from Havana the necessary questions and then agreed that we should talk, but allowing those people to enter without the door being opened. Fidel asked whether we had a ladder, and when I replied that we did, he directed that the speakers could enter the embassy via this ladder placed against the wall.

I quickly went to the garden. There on the grass was an aluminum ladder. I spotted one of our youngest officials, Elio Perrera, and gave him his task. With the help of others he climbed the wall, and sitting astride it, he began to communicate with those people who were interested in dialogue. When the mob saw him from the street they began to throw stones at him, to shout insults, and even told him that he had one foot in "freedom" and should come down. After agreeing to our proposal, one by one they climbed the ladder that Elio had placed on the outside of the wall. Thus, under conditions that we established, they entered our embassy.

Two officials from the Baruta and City councils came in first, with a police sergeant who left his weapon outside. They asked us if a TV channel could film the conversation as a witness. We agreed and some Canal Televen technicians came in. We sat down in the lobby and I asked them to explain what was going on. Just as I was beginning my comments, the mayor of Baruta, Henrique Capriles Radonski, and two companions—a young lawyer whom he brought as an advisor, and a slim, anxious woman who smoked continuously and was introduced as a member of the Civic Action Democratic Coordinating Committee—joined the talks. Later, Commissioner Henry Vivas, chief of the Metropolitan Police, entered by climbing the same aluminum ladder as the others.

In an arrogant and highhanded manner, Mayor Radonski and his civilian companions insisted again and again that we should allow them to check the embassy and consulate to determine whether Diosdado or any other asylum seekers were inside. Our response was unequivocal and precise: we rejected any form of pressure. We answered: "Cuba has the right to offer asylum to any person whom we consider requires it; nobody is sheltering in the embassy nor has any citizen requested that; international law is being flagrantly violated; and Mayor Radonski and the other authorities have allowed a highly dangerous situation to develop. Thus, it is up to him—and the other authorities—to stop the attack against us as soon as possible, without conditions, and to prevent any further violence erupting." We also stated, with a calm conviction, that we were prepared to defend Cuban sovereignty at the cost of our lives.

In the face of our firm positions, the mayor and his companions were obliged to leave the embassy and face the demands of the mob. Back in the street, somebody handed the loudspeaker to Radonski, who, still annoyed because he was unable to search the embassy, declared that he had been unable to do so because it was a diplomatic headquarters, implying that the supposed asylum seekers could indeed be there.

Both the mayor and the other council officials expressed their concern at what was happening. We could see that they were unsure of themselves. Then we discovered that they had received warnings from several Venezuelan public figures—many of whom we had contacted—on the negative political consequences for them of the barbarity that was being allowed. Any sensible observer—including members of the opposition and even certain people who backed the coup—could not ignore the international scandal that such events would provoke, and Cuba's right to react to the aggression to which it was being subjected.

That is why the Metropolitan Police subsequently brought in 40 troops to protect the embassy by forming a line on the sidewalk alongside the wall, thereby preventing individuals from trying to break into the entrance or jump the wall.

Meanwhile, as night fell, we reinforced the watch inside and assessed the minor improvement in the situation, maintaining our belief that anything could happen during the next few hours, particularly in the early hours of the morning. This was correct, because after Radonski left, the aggression of the mob did not diminish in any way.

When the mayor left the embassy, we took note of a comment Commissioner Henry Vivas had made. He had said: "We have information that the hillsides are beginning to move in a worrying manner."

Night fell, the shouting continued in the street, and through certain friends who called us on their cell phones, we learned that a fascist dictatorship had been proclaimed in Miraflores [Palace].

In darkness, with no water, and under blockade, at around 9:00 p.m. I was informed that Monsignor Baltazar Porras was outside the embassy and wished to see me. After taking appropriate precautions, given his status as a priest and his age, we opened the door so that he could enter normally. I immediately approached him, and to his shock, while we were greeting each other, two stones that could have fractured his skull landed on either side of him, within one meter of the outer wall of the embassy.

I said: "Monsignor, you are welcome, the stones speak for themselves, our words are not necessary; excuse me, we have no water or electricity, nor are they allowing food to be brought in, so we have to receive you in these precarious conditions and without any security. I thank you for the gesture of visiting us and hope that you are able to prevent the disrespect for international law and human rights." Within a few minutes, Henry Vivas joined us again. The Globovisión television channel asked to film the dialogue, and as both parties were in agreement, I told the journalist that we would prefer to talk alone and give interviews afterwards. That was what occurred. However, neither interview was transmitted; Porras's visit was not reported.

It should be noted that almost all of the Veneuelan media

condemned us from April 12 to April 15. After April 14, with honorable exceptions, events outside the embassy were not covered. In fact, a Globovisión journalist told me on April 12: "All of Venezuela knows what the Cubans think and we're not interested in that."

One month later, in a beautiful gesture, a group of young people headed by the filmmaker Angel Palacios made the documentary film "Siege of an Embassy," which was broadcast on several occasions by the state television channel and sold in kiosks on the streets of Caracas.

Almost at the beginning of the conversation with Monsignor Porras, Commissioner Henry Vivas called Mayor Alfredo Peña on his cell phone, who apparently wanted to talk to me. Although I had not yet spoken to our visitor, I explained the details to Mayor Peña with the intention of making him responsible for what was happening and the probable outcome. In our conversation, the monsignor was careful; at no point did he make any requests or insinuations, but he did gain a stronger sense of the need for urgent action. When he left, he addressed those present over the loudspeaker, dissuading them from continuing their actions and asking them to leave, provoking boos from many people.

By 11:00 p.m. the rabble had shrunk to almost half its former size and the shouting was only sporadic. At the same time, the thunderous roar of saucepan lids being banged by thousands of citizens clamoring for the return of the constitutional president could be heard from the populous barrios; tens of thousands outside the Tiuna Fortress were demanding the release of Chávez; and the people were preparing, virtually spontaneously, to come down from the hillsides and rescue Chávez on the following day, Saturday, April 13.

We were beginning to hear something of all this when, once again, before leaving the embassy with Monsignor Porras, Commissioner Vivas stated — this time without any subterfuge —

that it was urgent to settle the issue of the embassy, because he needed all his troops in the barrios to "neutralize" the popular mobilizations and the excesses of the "plunderers of businesses."

Around 11:00 p.m. an elegantly dressed General Damiani Bustillos made an appearance, after the ceremony in which Pedro Carmona had appointed him minister of the interior in his short-lived cabinet. I had met the general when he was head of the Defense Studies Institute, where I gave a lecture on Cuba every year. He tried to make the meeting cordial and recalled the two occasions on which he had received me there. He stated that he had instructions from Carmona to try to normalize the situation and had decided to pass by the embassy before participating in his daughter's wedding that night. I explained the situation to him and asked him to remove the people outside the embassy and to restore the water and electricity. He promised that he would do so. I observed that he was concerned about public opinion and he asked us to take the wrecked cars to the Metropolitan Police station, commenting: "That spectacle is pretty grotesque." I stated that everything that happened outside the embassy was his responsibility and that I would not raise any objections to the removal of the cars, but that he should also remove the people responsible for the damage. When Bustillos left, the number of people outside was smaller. He talked to them and asked them to respect the embassy.

April 13, 2002

During the early hours of the morning some of the cars were removed and the electricity and water services were restored. The attackers appeared to be retreating.

By 4:00 a.m. only some policemen and a young couple talking intimately under a streetlight remained on the street. Compañero Tomás Díaz went out to have a look at the desolate scene, and while he was checking out the wreckage of cars, rocks, cans, garbage and bottles, the wall painted with hostile slogans and other evidence of that hellish day, he approached the couple, who reacted curiously to the Cuban's words. He asked them how such a mess could have happened, and told them that there were children, women and men inside the embassy, that the water and electricity had been turned off and that no food had been allowed in. The young people looked ashamed and sincerely uncomfortable. They went off, and after a while, returned with a number of hamburgers.

Saturday April 13 dawned and the birds were singing. Looking out of a window at the vegetation on Mount Ávila as the sun came up, I felt in that vision of nature the continued blooming of life, and although the episode not yet over, I knew that we had won. In those first 24 hours after the coup we did not know what had happened and there was still no information on the whereabouts of President Chávez. Our own self-defense obliged us to concentrate our efforts on preserving our sovereignty and demonstrating to the fascists that Cuba had to be respected.

At 8:00 a.m. the initial provocateurs reappeared. The Metropolitan Police had mounted a cordon around the embassy and the front of the embassy was clear. In any case, we noticed that, as the morning passed, the number of people barely reached 30. "Something's going on," we said, while trying unsuccessfully to find out what was happening on television and radio.

At around 11:00 a.m. many friends began to call, telling us joyfully: "The people are in the streets, and Tiuna Fortress and Miraflores are surrounded by people!" Shortly afterwards, they told us that Miraflores had been taken by soldiers loyal to the president and that Carmona had been arrested.

I had just received this phone message when a compañero came running upstairs to tell us that the few remaining demonstrators had just dispersed, quickly followed by the Metropolitan Police.

Their departure finally confirmed that the fascist coup was being defeated. We continued to receive fresh information on what was happening. Everyone in the embassy felt that our victory was not isolated, because we had a premonition that the day would also bring the triumph of the Venezuelan people over fascism.

Still, we didn't drop our guard. And we were right not to, because at 5:00 p.m. that Saturday, in a final act of desperation, the fascists threw eight Molotov cocktails and four petrol bombs from a house behind the consulate, and the building almost caught on fire. Our compañeros in the consulate, a few meters from the embassy — three men and two women — acted heroically; they too suffered the onslaught of the fascist mob, their water and power were cut off and the fanatics tried on several occasions to enter the building.

April 14, 2002

All the efforts of the coup plotters had been in vain. Chávez was alive and heading for Miraflores, where the people and the soldiers who respected the constitution waited for him.

While this was going on, I decided to go home to share the good news with my wife and son and the other compañeros. Without intending to, I realized that I was following the same route that I had driven on April 11, but in the opposite direction. I thought: "That's a happy coincidence, because for the coup plotters, things have gone the other way."

The streets of the city looked like a cemetery on a moonless night. No voices could be heard and no lights were visible in many houses and apartments. While the car advanced, I imagined the rage and frustration of those who — barely 24 hours earlier — believed that they had managed to kill the dreams and halt the advance of the Bolivarian people. Many of them had been deceived by a minority well trained in lies and manipulation, who now, confused and shaken at the unexpected outcome, were mute.

Over five kilometers, I only saw one other car on the road. Its two occupants looked like waxwork figures. I switched on the radio; there was no news except on the state radio station, which continued to report the president's imminent return to the palace. I could hear the euphoric voices of the people crowded outside Miraflores, waiting for their leader. Then I was overcome and shouted out with great joy: "He's back, he's back, he's back!" — even though, I realized, Chávez had never left the soul of his noble and brave people, which is why, in record time, his enemies had to accept an ignominious defeat.

When I entered the residence, everyone came into the living room and began to applaud with great joy, and many people could not contain their tears when we sang the national anthem. I gave my son Carlos Ernesto and my wife Amarilys a hug and thanked them both, without having to say why. From the embassy, we had remained in contact with the residence and we were proud of the conduct of our compañeros, especially the children and teenagers.

I greeted each of my compañeros and they related their anecdotes: they told me that the children had slept in a bedroom selected to protect them from any possible aggression. The house resembled a war zone: everything in darkness, mattresses on the floor, compañeros on guard… Suddenly, I realized that I hadn't bathed in three days, so I decided to clean myself up before returning to the embassy. While I was showering, Amarilys continued recounting anecdotes. One story demonstrated the dignity and courage of our compañeros: one group wanted to go to the palace to burst in as the dictator Pedro Carmona proclaimed himself president and expose the fascist aggression against our embassy. Now, they reluctantly understood that the instructions they received not to go ahead with that plan were correct. The conduct of everyone there was exemplary.

Just as I was leaving Fidel Castro rang from Havana to find

out how long we thought it would be before Chávez returned to Caracas. I could sense that he was exhausted and anxious, but happy on account of the epic victory of the Bolivarian people. From the morning of April 11, Fidel was in continual phone communication with us. We received his directions at every moment, and even his constant questions were heartening and a formidable stimulus for confronting whatever might happen.

Back at the embassy, around 3:00 a.m. we were brought up to date. Osvaldo Parlá reminded us that the day before, Saturday, was the birthday of Marcel, the young son of our compañero Felipe Gil. That was it, a bottle of rum appeared from somewhere, we sang happy birthday, we hugged each other and repeated as a joke that Marcel, and maybe all of us, had been born for the second time. And then I paused to consider that the Bolivarian Republic was itself being "born again."

When we went out into the street on that memorable morning of Sunday, April 14, the light was so intense that all traces of the barbarity had disappeared. Suddenly, we were surprised by a happy and noisy convoy of Venezuelan brothers and sisters, including the Venezuelan ambassador to Cuba, Julio Montes, who, at Miraflores Palace, had been prepared to give his life for the Bolivarian revolution. When he saw us, we melted together in a huge embrace.

Then, in the same spot where hours earlier the fascists had shouted their threats, the voices of the people chanted: "He's back! He's back! Chávez is back!"

One of the members of that convoy told us that they had come to make amends, saying: "As in the times of Martí and Bolívar, Cuba and Venezuela are once again demonstrating that it is only possible to win with reason and the strength of the people." We applauded him and exclaimed in unison: "Long live Cuba! Long live Venezuela!"

Since those April days, I have seen and have been able to feel in the thousands of Venezuelans who approached us to apologize the grandeur and honor of this unconquerable people. The siege and aggression against our embassy contributed to revealing the sinister face of fascism, and since that siege and aggression was part of the plot to implant fascism in Venezuela, our modest resistance, to the honor of the Cuban people, was associated with the crushing and heroic victory of the Venezuelan patriots.

Talks in defense of the homeland

Talks with Mayor Henrique Capriles Radonski and those accompanying him during the siege of the Cuban embassy.

Some time after 3:00 p.m. on April 12, 2002, the mob of more than 1,000 people in the street outside the embassy began to chant that they were giving a one-hour ultimatum for the diplomatic headquarters to be opened up, or they would take it by force. In that tense and dangerous atmosphere, we heard the voices of some officials who, amid the tumult, were asking for dialogue and shouting that they wished to avoid violence. For their part, Salvador Romaní and Ricardo Koesling, the two principal leaders of the mob, were inciting the crowd not to wait any longer.

In that context, we decided to engage in such talks, without knowing the identity of the public officials involved. In the midst of the prevailing chaos, it seemed to us that we should not reject any possibility of preventing the individuals manipulating that violent mob from succeeding in their objective of gaining forced entry into our embassy and thus unleashing a situation of disastrous consequences, given our unequivocal decision to defend with our lives the integrity and dignity of the representation of the Cuban state and people in Venezuela.

At the risk of his life, speaking from the top of the wall, Elio

Perrera, an embassy official, invited those interested in dialogue to enter the headquarters.

By means of a ladder, the two representatives of Baruta and City councils climbed the wall and entered the embassy. Half an hour later, Mayor Capriles Radonski and two companions joined them; finally, Police Commissioner Henry Vivas arrived. Before beginning the talks, they asked for the presence—as witness—of a television crew, to which we agreed. The prevailing censorship prevented those talks being made public. We were only able to obtain a copy of the tape days later, and although it was mutilated in certain sections, it largely covered what happened during those two hours. The transcript is being made public here for the first time.

* * *

Germán Sánchez: First and foremost, we would like you to explain the reasons for the presence here outside the embassy of this group of Venezuelan citizens. For some hours, those people have been making demands and yelling obscenities, and they have even destroyed several vehicles that have diplomatic immunity— a serious crime in any country of the world. Moreover, they are threatening to enter the embassy by force.

I am convinced that the majority of those citizens are not aware of the gravity of forcibly entering this—or any other— diplomatic headquarters, and that it would be a violation of the sovereignty and integrity of Cuban national territory. According to international law—particularly the regulations of the Vienna Convention—states are bound to protect the integrity of diplomatic missions. This is an inviolable principle that all states are obliged to fulfill, it is a sacred tenet of international law.

If an embassy is violated by citizens of the country in which it functions, it is the national authorities' responsibility.

Those of us in this mission feel as if we are in our homeland,

and like you Venezuelans, we Cubans love our homeland. And thus we are going to defend this piece of Cuba to the end.

At this point, what we want is to clarify what has provoked this dangerous situation. It is something that we do not understand, and of course this conversation is between people who wish to understand each other and to avert the grave consequences that will follow if Cuba's sovereignty is violated.

You should also know that there are children and women in our headquarters; we are all civilian workers fulfilling a diplomatic mission in Venezuela. We do not involve ourselves in Venezuela's internal affairs. We are respectful of the authorities. We have had recourse to them constantly throughout the day; we have been making proposals for some hours now to prevent the people in this mission being affected, and of course, to stop those who are attempting to invade this Cuban soil.

Representative of the City council: You have spoken about the law, we respect the law and your sovereignty and I apologize for the violence and destruction of the cars. We have suffered damage for three years; we have suffered damage to the morale and the lives of Venezuelans. We are here, simply, because there are people here that have violated the law.

Germán Sánchez: Which people?

Representative of the City council: The people who, allegedly, are here and in the consulate.

Germán Sánchez: Ah! That is the issue!

Representative of Baruta council: I would like to clarify things with the ambassador because here we have dealt with an issue that I think is important. In terms of the Cuban embassy, everything is going to be safeguarded, both people and property. Things got a bit out of hand, like the destruction of the vehicles, which I know enjoy diplomatic immunity; but they were not identified by their license plates and it was not possible to determine whether they were private or diplomatic.

We are going to fulfill the international agreements signed by the Venezuelan government. The only thing that we want is, first, a clarification as to whether there are Venezuelan citizens within the Cuban embassy. Second, we would like you to clarify for us if you are prepared to give asylum to Venezuelan citizens who request it of the Cuban government.

[*At this point Mayor Radonski and two companions arrive.*]

Germán Sánchez: Well, I will start with your second question. If you know anything of international law, you must know that the right exists both in Venezuela and in Cuba to assess any citizen who requests political asylum. That is valid in any diplomatic headquarters in Latin America. It is an agreement binding on all states in the region. You are a lawyer, right? Then surely you know that this is a sacred principle in Latin America, which has a tradition dating back several decades. Thus your question can only have one response: "We would do the same as Venezuela, Brazil or any other Latin American country."

On the first question, I can categorically affirm that no Venezuelan citizen is here at the diplomatic mission of Cuba in Venezuela. And moreover, I will add that no Venezuelan citizen has requested asylum in our embassy. We can say this with the authority of an ambassador and the respect merited by a diplomatic site.

Publicly, and before the opinion of the entire world, and of course, the Venezuelan people — this is being recorded — I can affirm that no Venezuelan citizen is being sheltered in this embassy. The rumors are totally false.

Representative of Baruta council: And what of the neighbors who are saying that they saw a car in which Diosdado Cabello, Iris Varela and Nicolás Maduro entered the embassy?

Germán Sánchez: I would suggest that you ask the neighbors whether they can be sure that that was the case, because I heard that story from a Venezuelan journalist (Marta Colomina), but now you are here and the most appropriate thing you could do is talk to the neighbors, find the neighbors who said that they have seen Diosdado Cabello, bring them here before us and let them say that to our faces. And, as proof, place a television camera close to the embassy for as long as you want. That is Venezuelan territory, you have the right to do so, and they will confirm, one day, that the story is untrue.

Mayor Radonski's assistant: On behalf of Venezuela, the civil society, democratic people, honest people, the people who live in harmony, we wish to tell you that Venezuela is going to fulfill the international obligations governing diplomatic relations. That means that the immunity and privileges, both of the head of the Cuban delegation, yourself, and of other members — and their property — are going to be respected.

At the same time, I have to tell you that it is necessary that the Venezuelan people can confirm from a serious source, from a real source, that none of the people that we mentioned are here. Ambassador, we need real proof, we need to know that the people whom we presumed to be here are not here. We need absolute sincerity, we need to inform those people shouting outside, because we do not want acts of violence; what we want is a bit of harmony and respect for international regulations that are law in Venezuela.

I ask you, ambassador, that by whatever means you choose, you let us know if a member of the former cabinet of the government of Lieutenant Colonel Hugo Chávez is here.

Germán Sánchez: Would anyone like to add anything else?

Mayor Radonski's second assistant: Yes. I am a member of the Civic Action Democratic Coordinating Committee. One year ago, we organized a protest outside the Cuban embassy. Moreover, as a teacher, I proposed that it should take place at a certain distance from the embassy, as I am respectful of international law. So there I was, outside the embassy. And I was followed twice. I was with a woman who participated in that demonstration: Irma Máez, whom I met that day; we were surrounded by the Bolivarian circles; it was the first time that I felt the violence of the Bolivarian circles, armed, abusive, and I asked myself what is happening here, because Venezuela is not a country of hatred. I worked on the Deputies Foreign Policy Commission 10 years ago and received delegations from the Cuban government and the opposition. And I want you to know about the kidnapping and torture of Irma Máez by 14 people, who all spoke like Cubans and insulted her, asking her for information because she was a member of the Institutional Military Front, and asking if she was conspiring against the government. We were against the government because we believe in democracy and freedom.

And what I experienced yesterday, the 11th… yesterday I was one block from Miraflores and we were massacred by snipers. I don't want violence but those people outside are reacting to what happened yesterday. It has been said and repeated — thousands of times — that there are "seedbeds" of violence which have the support of Cuba. And if those people who have instigated the violence are here, like Iris Varela, whom I was told was here, and also Diosdado Cabello, you should not give them political asylum. My question is if you would give political asylum to those people.

Germán Sánchez: I would like to reiterate that it is an irrevocable principle that every state has the authority to decide whom it will shelter and whom it will not shelter.

In the first place, it must be clarified to those Venezuelan men and women outside the embassy that they are outside a diplomatic headquarters, which is the territory of a sovereign country, and has to be respected. Perhaps those people we hear constantly shouting are not aware that if they attack this embassy, as they are threatening to do shortly—or any other embassy—the representatives of that nation will react as the Cuban people do when they are attacked by another country. There is no middle ground! There is no other possibility! It is important that they know that. Very important. Of course, we do not want any blood spilt, totally the opposite. We love the Venezuelan people very much, as if they were our own people; the historical reasons are well known.

What is needed now is for someone to explain very concretely to those people that they are being manipulated. We know some of the provocateurs. One of them arrived very early on: Ricardo Koesling, the very man who some time ago spoke of 1,500 Cuban agents in Venezuela led by a super-agent. It was quickly confirmed that this was a great lie, fabricated for electoral purposes.

I would like you to know, Mayor Radonski, that at this time our embassy has no electricity or water. This headquarters is being attacked, as we were attacked 40 years ago by the United States, and we have never made a concession to any empire, or to anyone who imposes himself by force on our country. It must be explained to those people that we are talking in a civilized manner, and that violence always has a lamentable outcome. The violence started here with the destruction of our cars, strikes on our doors, throwing of Molotov cocktails, and threats that they will take over the embassy. Ricardo Koesling made this threat in front of a Baruta police officer, before an authority of this council. And that policeman—we can confirm it—communicated with his superiors and informed them that there were threats that the embassy was going to be assaulted. People have continued arriving, many of them confused, manipulated by a small group, which clearly wants and is seeking bloodshed. We cannot be naive, neither you nor ourselves! You have acknowledged that a diplomatic head-quarters must be respected.

Those people outside must know that too, because they are being encouraged to enter violently through that door, which will oblige us to react as our people do if attacked. We would defend this piece of land with our lives! These are not just words. We Cubans do not make empty speeches. We have demonstrated that many times. I invite you to avert a tragedy! It is in your hands, mayor. There are children here as well as women; we are being attacked, our electricity has been cut off, our water has been cut off; here there are children, men and women who are going to be hungry! Why? What right do they have to act in that manner? Is that a just, humanitarian, democratic, sincere way to act?

My word is the word of a people and is the word of a state. In everything that I have said here, I have been as we Cubans always are, clear and precise. You have asked me questions and I have responded. There are no Venezuelans being sheltered here. If that is the pretext used by certain people to provoke an act of violence with incalculable consequences, that pretext must be eliminated. It must disappear. If they continue to provoke those people into protesting against this embassy on the basis of a false pretext, history and the international community will judge harshly those responsible: yourselves, especially yourselves, the authorities of both councils. Moreover, we have informed the Venezuelan Foreign Ministry via a diplomatic note; we have informed Efraín Vázquez Velazco, chief of the army. We have also informed the nuncio, various Venezuelan public figures and various embassies. This is a situation with potentially grave consequences for the international community, and most particularly, for the people who are here and in the consulate. You should meditate on what is happening and avoid a tragic outcome.

Mayor Radonski: Allow me, ambassador. The first thing that I want to say is that I am not going to raise a single gun or a single pistol against the people out there. I want to say that in the best possible way. I am not going to do what was done in Venezuela yesterday, which was to shoot. Ambassador, I was shot at yesterday. I was not waving a gun around; I was on a peaceful protest, because in democratic regimes people have the possibility of expressing what they want...

Germán Sánchez: Mayor, please excuse me interrupting. To date, this demonstration outside the embassy has not been peaceful; on the contrary, it has been very violent.

We have been attacked since the early hours of the morning. There have been acts of violence here. They have destroyed cars belonging to this embassy, they have struck that door and they are shouting that they are going to enter this mission by force. At this moment, we are under the threat of an ultimatum.

Thus the situation that has been created includes violence, and hence our great concern; it is for that reason that we agreed to this dialogue, in order to avert an outbreak of violence on the part of those who are outside demonstrating. As the highest authority in this municipality, this would be your responsibility. Of course, it would also be the responsibility of all the Venezuelan authorities in charge of protecting diplomatic headquarters. Last year, when there was an anti-Cuban demonstration, you called me and guaranteed that it would only be allowed at a distance that did not endanger our security.

Regrettably, on this occasion, what has happened has gone beyond your control, and when a group of hundreds of people is incited to violence, it can be provoked.

[*There is a short interruption in the recording.*]

I invite you to find an immediate solution and avoid this getting out of hand.

Mayor Radonski: I agree that diplomatic headquarters must be protected. At no point did I give orders for the electricity to be cut off here…

Germán Sánchez: So who cut it off?

Mayor Radonski: Well, I don't know, I don't know.

Germán Sánchez: It is important to find out who did it, because there have been flagrant violations of the law here in front of the Baruta authorities and the TV cameras. It is very important to know the identity of the people stating that the entry of food is going to be prevented, and that they are going to take over the Cuban embassy. It is very important to know who those people are.

Mayor Radonski: I am going to say something, ambassador: when you give a party here, you open up the embassy. People move around inside the embassy headquarters and share everything. Appealing to your intelligence, we have not come here to doubt your word, because yes, there are going to be many reports about comings and goings. But—if you want—I think that this could be settled now if you allow us to check the embassy, so we can tell the people outside that we have confirmed that neither Diosdado Cabello nor any other Venezuelan is being sheltered in the embassy. Look, the US ambassador invited me to visit his embassy and he showed me over the headquarters, I was able to tour it with him…

Germán Sánchez: [*Interrupts.*] Excuse me, if I invite you into this embassy in the same way that many Venezuelans enter every day under normal conditions, that would be a different matter. But what I cannot accept—and I do not believe that any ambassador would accept it—is having my territory checked, my word doubted, the word of someone who is representing their people. You have the right to take these cameras and install them outside the embassy for centuries. Then, the truth will be confirmed. But, what is inadmissible in terms of honor and dignity and international principles, is what you are asking us. That is inadmissible...

[*Recording interrupted.*]

Venezuelans and Cubans have been brothers for centuries, united by innumerable events. Thus it is absurd that acts of violence that could lead to an extreme situation should be carried out by these people, the majority of whom—I am absolutely convinced—are being manipulated by an extremely small group of individuals. I insist: if the issue is the alleged presence of any Venezuelan here, that pretext is totally false. I repeat that so that you can reflect on it.

[*Recording interrupted. At this point, the representatives of the Baruta and City councils insist on the need to inspect the embassy.*]

Germán Sánchez: You are here without electricity. We haven't even been able to offer you a drink of water. We haven't even been able to offer you a coffee, and that is not discourtesy on our part: we have no water and cannot make coffee. That is a violation! That is pressure! That is an insult! That is an international scandal!

You are asking me something—to allow an inspection of this embassy—and with total respect I will respond to you: that is not laid down in the regulations covering the right to asylum. Let me say this: You are all educated and informed people. I am conversing with you because you are the representatives of that group of people who are outside, and I do so with much pleasure. We have taken this step to try to avoid what a small, violent, unthinking, manipulative group is seeking.

Mayor Radonski: Let me make one thing clear. I cannot fire even one teargas grenade to disperse the people.

Germán Sánchez: But they can violate the integrity of this embassy? They are already beginning to do so! They have already done so! Please understand me, we have been here for hours without water, without electricity!

[*At this point we are informed that Commissioner Henry Vivas, chief of the Metropolitan Police, is on his way.*]

Germán Sánchez: Please, come in and join us in discussing these issues.

Mayor Radonski: Look, ambassador, let me finish...

Germán Sánchez: [*Interrupts.*] When will the power be reconnected? When will the water supply be reestablished? What is happening here at this moment is an international embarrassment! It is against ethical, humanitarian principles! A democrat, a humanist, cannot allow children to be without electricity or water or food!

Baruta official: We will commit ourselves to restoring the water and electricity as soon as possible. We cannot do that ourselves. We have to ask the companies to do it.

Germán Sánchez: Who cut them off?

Baruta official: We do not know.

Germán Sánchez: And how has this situation gotten out of your hands? This is like throwing teargas at innocent people. It is exactly the same. It has already happened in front of the authorities of this council! There were police here! We have informed them, as I told you, and it is still going on!

Representative of Baruta council: We trust in your word, but we must insist on inspecting the embassy. If you wish, invite the nuncio to accompany us.

[*Commissioner Henry Vivas joins the conversation.*]

Germán Sánchez: [*Summarizes for Vivas what has happened.*]

Mayor Radonski: Ambassador, what are you proposing?

Germán Sánchez: I am proposing that you fulfill your duty, which is, in the first place, to speak with those people outside, to tell them that they have the right to be there for the rest of their lives. If they wish, other people may replace them. If they are in any doubt, that is their right. They are on Venezuelan territory. And we have the right and the duty to say exactly how things are.

But the harassment of the embassy, attacks on vehicles, striking on the door, blocking the free movement of officials, threatening a violent attack on our headquarters, and trying to set fire to them, are acts that are way beyond international law!

These acts of violence started four days ago—during the night of April 9. I should inform you that before the acts of violence of yesterday, April 11, there was firing in the air a few meters away in the street, a Molotov cocktail was thrown into the entrance to the embassy, and some tires were also burned.

Mayor Radonski: I am a political figure, the Baruta police and the Metropolitan Police are guaranteeing that nobody is going to scale that wall.

Germán Sánchez: But, right now, they are not able to guarantee it, if those people decide to do so.

Henry Vivas: I am guaranteeing it to you.

Germán Sánchez: You cannot, how many police do you have here?

Henry Vivas: I already have 40 police officers.

Germán Sánchez: That is not sufficient.

Henry Vivas: For me, that is sufficient.

Germán Sánchez: And how are you going to do it? We cannot permit violence outside our embassy, sticks, blows, injuries, whatever. That would be very sad!

I am asking you in a constructive tone to find a solution. It is absolutely up to you. We have agreed to this dialogue in the spirit of avoiding bloodshed, of avoiding disastrous consequences. I am urging you to communicate with the national authorities, who have the responsibility — together with yourselves — to solve this problem.

6. Some concluding remarks about Hugo Chávez

The following is an excerpt of remarks made by the author to Cuban journalists Rosa Miriam Elizalde and Luis Báez for their book El Encuentro *(The Meeting), published in 2004.*

I arrived in Venezuela in August 1994 with the mission of developing Cuba's diplomatic relations and, in particular, commercial and economic links with this country. I was also to prioritize the promotion of Cuban services in the scientific, health, educational, athletic and cultural fields.

I was aware that Venezuela and Cuba enjoy a common historical and cultural identity, a geographic closeness, and sympathy between the two peoples, which could only favor the work of any diplomat. Of course, significant hurdles were also obvious, such as the alliance of then-President Rafael Caldera with the US government, and his friendship with the leaders of the Cuban-American mafia organizations.

Before leaving for Venezuela, I proposed to immediately seek contact with Hugo Chávez, whom we hardly knew in Cuba, but whom we admired on account of the uprising he led on February 4, 1992...

In my first conversation, I observed that Hugo — that is what he asked me to call him — did not have a clear idea of how to achieve power, but he revealed a certainty that he was going to achieve it.

His confidence in the majority of Venezuela's soldiers and his love and fidelity toward his people caught my attention. I was moved by his desire to revive the legacy of Bolívar and he devoted a large part of the conversation to the question of how to promote — in our time — the historical project of the Anfictiónico Congress.

After my first meeting with Chávez, barely one month after having arrived in Caracas, I felt quite a personal political curiosity at knowing a unique leader who had arisen at the worst moment for the left and the popular movements in our continent and the rest of the world. I couldn't forget that the Soviet Union had disappeared in August 1991 after its allies in Eastern Europe had collapsed in 1989. Almost simultaneously, the Sandinistas lost power in Nicaragua and the revolutionary processes in El Salvador and Guatemala were stalled. Meanwhile, in South America, Mexico and part of the Caribbean, the left was making a determined effort — although almost always in a defensive manner — to construct alternative programs and to accumulate the necessary forces to face the terrible advance of neoliberalism and the overwhelming offensive of the United States...

I was fascinated by Chávez's eloquence, the freshness of his ideas and his luminous conviction that he would succeed in leading his people back on the course of Bolívar...

A new stage of hope and redemption for the peoples of our America began with Chávez and the Bolivarian revolution, and since 1992, at the historical moment in which it was most needed, the social struggles and the struggles of the left in our continent have been revitalized.

After 10 years, like many other people, I know and admire Chávez more and understand him better. During this decade that I have lived in Venezuela, I have come closer to the glorious history of the Venezuelan people, and have come to understand the paradoxes of this country: its enormous wealth largely appropriated by a tiny oligarchy at the cost of the extreme poverty of the majority; a burning injustice that contrasts with the virtues of the Bolivarian people—a rebellious, fighting, noble people with exceptional intelligence and instincts. Without understanding this Venezuelan society in which both inequality and a heroic history are manifest, it is impossible to comprehend the leader that is Hugo Chávez. He is a loving person, totally in solidarity with the dispossessed, as simple and vast as the plains where he was born; the prodigal and loyal son of Barinas and an honorable and dignified Venezuela.

If 10 years ago I found it hard to categorize Chávez, I now feel capable of agreeing with many people who see in him a leader with an immense, fully developed creative ability; a revolutionary commander-in-chief who sprang from his people and who, unlike anyone else in Venezuela, has been able to give new life to Bolívar, Miranda, Robinson, Sucre, Zamora, Martí and Che—his most admired predecessors. From them, with his own example and lucidity, he has encouraged the awakening of his nation. Chávez succeeded in doing what Bolívar could not do in his time, and what Martí demanded afterwards: "Chip the teeth of the ungrateful." Chávez understands that his invincible power will always come from the pain and the love that he feels for the poor of his land and of other lands; moreover, he knows, thanks to those years of struggle, where his enemies and his allies lie, within and outside of Venezuela. That makes us trust in him even more…

What most impresses me about Chávez these days is his *joie de vivre* and his spontaneous way of infecting others with his smile; at the same time, he is occasionally overwhelmed by profound anguish because he cannot eradicate poverty more quickly. He has stated that the worst enemies of the revolution are also within it, and that formidable undertakings are needed to transform the material and mental structures of the old regime that remain very powerful and active. I am convinced that this captivating and iconoclastic human being, both fierce and tender, will lead his people to a complete victory.

His choice to lead an exemplary austere and generous life, devoted to serving the poor and all human beings committed to honor and equality, will remain crucial.

The solidarity Chávez has shown in relations with Cuba since 1994 is also noteworthy... When his adversaries in Venezuela accused him of imitating Cuba and Fidel, he was more valiant than ever. Far from severing his links with our country, he included Cuba as a beneficiary of the Caracas Energy Agreement and signed a Cooperation Agreement with Fidel that initiated the fuller and accelerated integration that exists today among the peoples of the region.

Those who twisted Chávez's words at the University of Havana in November 1999, when he described Cuba and Venezuela as advancing toward the same "sea of happiness," could not imagine that that is how it would be. As Chávez himself noted at the time, each country is advancing in its own way, but both more than ever in the defense and the realization of the ideas of Bolívar and Martí.

Caracas, November 23, 2004

ALSO FROM OCEAN PRESS

LATIN AMERICA AT THE CROSSROADS
Domination, Crisis, Popular Movements, and Political Alternatives
Roberto Regalado

A comprehensive analysis of contemporary Latin American politics and the deepening conflict between the region and the US at the beginning of the 21st century. This up-to-date account presents an analysis of recent events including coca farmer Evo Morales's electoral victory in Bolivia and the escalating conflict between Venezuela's President Chávez and Washington.

ISBN 978-1-920888-71-8 (Also available in Spanish ISBN 978-1-921235-00-9)

SALVADOR ALLENDE READER
Chile's Voice of Democracy
Edited with an introduction by James D. Cockcroft

On September 11, 1973, General Augusto Pinochet led a bloody coup against President Salvador Allende in Chile. Allende died in the Presidential Palace as it was attacked by Pinochet's army. Controversy still surrounds the role of Washington and the CIA in the overthrow of the popularly elected government of Allende, a self-proclaimed Marxist.

This first-ever anthology presents Allende's voice and his vision of a more democratic, peaceful and just world to a new generation.

ISBN 978-1-876175-24-5

CHILE: THE OTHER SEPTEMBER 11
An Anthology of Reflections on the 1973 Coup
Ariel Dorfman, Salvador Allende, Pablo Neruda, Victor Jara, Fidel Castro et al.

Reflecting on another day of terror and tragedy, this anthology includes Ariel Dorfman's poignant essay, "The Last September 11," poetry by Pablo Neruda, the song composed by Victor Jara just before his brutal murder, and President Allende's final radio broadcast to the nation.

ISBN 978-1-920888-44-2 (Also available in Spanish ISBN 978-1-920888-81-7)

CHE: A MEMOIR BY FIDEL CASTRO
Edited by David Deutschmann

Fidel Castro writes with great candor and emotion about a historic revolutionary partnership that changed the face of Cuba and Latin America, vividly portraying Che—the man, the revolutionary, and the intellectual—and revealing much about his own inimitable determination and character.

This new edition includes Fidel's speech on the return of Che's remains to Cuba 30 years after his assassination in Bolivia in 1967, and provides a frank assessment of the Bolivian mission.

ISBN 978-1-920888-25-1 (Also available in Spanish ISBN 978-1-921235-02-3)

ALSO FROM OCEAN PRESS

FIDEL CASTRO READER

Edited by Deborah Shnookal and David Deutschmann

The voice of one of the 20th century's most controversial political figures—and most outstanding orators—is captured in this unique selection of Castro's key speeches over 50 years.

Fidel Castro has been an articulate and penetrating—if controversial—political thinker and leader, who has outlasted 10 hostile US presidents. With the wave of change now sweeping the continent, this book sheds light on Latin America's past as well as its future.

ISBN 978-1-920888-88-6

CHE GUEVARA READER
Writings on Politics and Revolution
Edited by David Deutschmann

The best-selling *Che Guevara Reader* is the most complete selection of Che Guevara's writings, letters, and speeches available in English.

ISBN 978-1-876175-69-6 (Also available in Spanish ISBN 978-1-876175-93-1)

CUBAN REVOLUTION READER
A Documentary History of Fidel Castro's Revolution
Edited by Julio García Luís

This new edition covering nearly 50 years of the Cuban revolution presents a comprehensive overview of key events in Cuba, the revolution's impact in Latin America and Africa, and Cuba's relations with the United States.

ISBN 978-1-920888-89-3 (Also available in Spanish ISBN 978-1-920888-08-4)

JOSÉ MARTÍ READER
Writings on the Americas

An elegant anthology featuring bilingual poetry, a revised translation and several new pieces. It presents the full breadth of Martí's work: his political essays and writings on culture, his letters and his poetry. Readers will discover a literary genius and an insightful political commentator on troubled US-Latin America relations.

ISBN 978-1-920888-74-9

LATIN AMERICA
Awakening of a Continent
Ernesto Che Guevara

This anthology presents Che Guevara's vision of Latin America, from his youthful travels until his death in Bolivia.

ISBN 978-1-920888-38-1 (Also available in Spanish ISBN 978-1-876175-71-9)

ALSO FROM OCEAN PRESS

CHÁVEZ
Venezuela and the New Latin America
Hugo Chávez, interviewed by Aleida Guevara

Elected by overwhelming popular mandate in 1998, Hugo Chávez is now one of Latin America's most outspoken political figures. This book documents an extraordinary interview between Chávez and Aleida Guevara, daughter of the legendary Che Guevara and a prominent figure in today's antiglobalization movement. Over the course of an extended, exclusive interview, Chávez explained his fiercely nationalist vision for Venezuela, the worldwide significance of the Bolivarian revolution, and his commitment to a united Latin America. Their conversation covered Chávez's personal political formation and the legacy of Che's ideas and example in Latin America today.

Also included is an interview with Jorge García Carneiro, the former minister of defense in Venezuela who played a key role in defeating the April 2002 coup attempt.

ISBN 978-1-920888-00-8 (Also available in Spanish ISBN 978-1-920888-22-0)

ALSO AVAILABLE: THE DVD

Featuring Aleida Guevara's interviews with Hugo Chávez and Jorge García Carneiro as well as vox-pops with Venezuelans involved in the country's many social programs, this documentary affords a rare opportunity to glimpse into a country rich with hope, dreams and... oil.

ISBN 978-1-920888-50-3 (Spanish with English subtitles)

"This is a different Venezuela, where the wretched of the earth know that they can free themselves from their past. And this is a different Latin America."
—Hugo Chávez

oceanpress

e-mail info@oceanbooks.com.au
www.oceanbooks.com.au